WOMEN OF WEIKERT

also by Emilie Freer Jansma —

*The Community of Weikert, PA —
Cabins and Camps, Homes and Homesteads*

*60 Oral History Interview Tapes of West End Residents
recorded by Louise Goehring Scott*

Hironimus Union Church
(late 19th cent.)

Women of Weikert

❧❦

Emilie Freer Jansma

EDITIONS
enlaplage

State College, Penna.

Published by Editions Enlaplage
State College, Pennsylvania
www.enlaplage.com

ISBN: 978-1-936466-15-3

© 2017 Emilie Freer Jansma

All rights reserved. No part of this volume may be reproduced without written permission of the publisher.

Cover photograph of Hattie Bogar Bilger courtesy of Caroline Bilger Wenrick. Background is a railroad quilt made for the author in 1991 by Genevieve Weaser of Weikert from pieces cut by Darla Cunningham.

10 9 8 7 6 5 4 3 2

printed by *Lulu*

Contents

List of Abbreviations viii

Acknowledgments ix

Map of the West End of Union County, PA xi

Foreword 1

Women of Weikert, circa 1820 to 2012 21

Timeline of Local and National Events 143

Social and Economic Influences on Weikert Life 145

Bibliography 149

Geographical and Thematic Index 153

Index of Personal Names 157

List of Abbreviations

b.	=	born
bap.	=	baptized
bur.	=	buried
CCC	=	Civilian Conservation Corps
Co	=	County
d.	=	died
dau.	=	daughter
div.	=	divorced
F.A.G.	=	Find A Grave (www.findagrave.com)
mar.	=	married
N....	=	unknown name
PA	=	Pennsylvania
Twsp	=	Township
UMC	=	United Methodist Church

Acknowledgments

I wish to thank all the people of the "West End" of Union County, Pennsylvania, particularly those folk who were born or raised in Hartley Township, who shared with me their memories, pictures, and family lore.

I wish to acknowledge the following people and their contributions to the book: Connie Wirt Bastian, Jane Ely Foster, Kitty Everett Frederick, and George "Jerry" Sholter, Jr., for the sharing of their family pictures and stories; Tim Bastian for his computer searches for pictures, articles, and death certificates of the subjects; Darla and Bill Cunningham for their photographs of the tombstones in the Hironimus Cemetery; Joyce Winn Landis, Mary Belle Lontz, the late Louise Goehring Scott, and the late Judy Shively Wagner, for their earlier historical works about the "West End;" the late Leona Sholter Wirt for her dozens of letters answering my many Weikert questions; the staff and volunteers of the Union County Historical Society; and the staff of the West End Library in Laurelton.

As with previous works of mine, this is also dedicated to the two Weikert women who were my mentors, Genevieve Friggle Weaser and Betty Kissinger Reich Snook. Then as now, I gave thanks for the support of my projects to Joan Maxine Auten, Bobbie Barnett Cronin, Jeanne Volinsky Eckrod, Mary Lou Kline Engle, Jean Dotts Jolly, Marion Fillmore Kahley, Alma Heizenroth Klauger, and Helen Irvine Klauger. In addition, for this volume I will add Judy Blair, M. Lillian Davenport, Donna Kahley Gemberling, Maryann Gaston Losik, Seth and Cathy Snyder Neuhauser, Janice Dorman Shively, Herb and Connie Snook Teichman, Caroline Bilger Wenrick, and Geri Bettilyon Willen.

In addition, these special men: Carl R. Catherman, Forrest Wenrick, Jonathan Bastian, Bob Jolly, Bruce Fisher, Corky Landis, Charles Klauger, and August "Pop" Barnett.

I extend my appreciation and gratitude for their warm hospitality, encouragement, and deep and abiding friendship, to Tony and Janice Dorman Shively and Dallas, Matt and Toni Jordan Klauger. No publications of mine would have been possible without my having had access to Tony Shively's life-long collection of western Union County historical materials.

I was most fortunate to have Donald Charles Jackman of enlaplage.com as my publisher, but even more to have him as my "book shepherd."

*This book is dedicated to all of the
Women of Weikert,
Union County, Pennsylvania,
past and present*

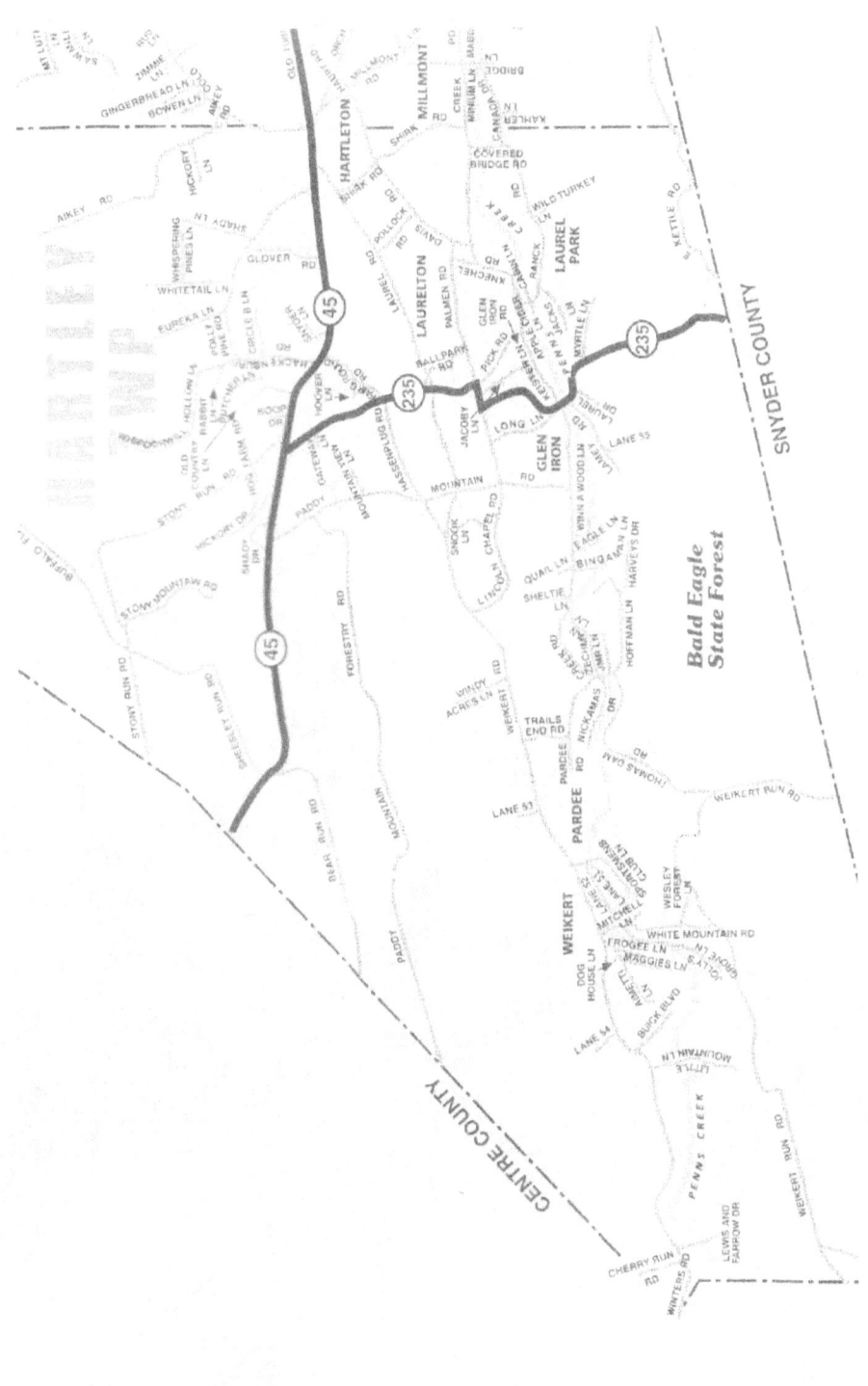

Foreword

This book is a beginning effort to recognize the past women of Weikert, Pennsylvania. It reflects my observations and opinions. By compiling and sharing this information, I hope to partially fill the void of what is known about these women and to add dimension and depth to the history of the "West End" of Union County. Sadly, often heretofore, the only remnant of a woman's existence has been her name chiseled into a rough gravestone.

Since 1975, I have been gathering bits and pieces of family stories and folklore. A limited amount of data comes from prime source documents. Many hours were spent searching in court house records and historical societies, sitting at kitchen tables in family homes, and tramping through cold windy churchyards.

Attempts to gather specific information was frequently frustrating, but at the same time very rewarding. It was often difficult to locate surviving family members who could provide information or pictures of the subjects, to find specific dates for happenings and events, and to identify which Ann, Anne, or Annie of which William Sr., William Jr., or William C. was being referred to. No attempts have been made "to prove" that any one story or "set of facts" is any more correct than any other, and the material is definitely subject to error. Inaccuracies may also have occurred during the information gathering and word processing.

In addition, a relatively few items have been omitted to respect the privacy of certain living individuals and their families. Any additions or corrections would be welcomed by the compiler. To those who were kind enough to provide pictures, occasionally the figures were too small or too indistinct to be reproduced, and on certain tombstone photos the information could not be read.

While many names in the Weikert area have had many spellings, I have not tried to force unified spelling for such as Bettelyon, Bettilyon, Bethlehem or the many ways Hironimus has appeared. Rather, I have used what was used by the particular writer on documents, newspaper articles, letters etc. at the time they were written. It has made the extensive indexing even more challenging.

My hopes are that this information will benefit and be of interest to others. The book is compiled for the "general reader," not necessarily for historians or academicians. The information is true and complete to the best of my knowledge. It is offered without guarantees on the part of the compiler and the publisher.

Weikert, sometimes called "the Tight End" or "the West End" of Hartley Township in Union County, is described even today in The Comprehensive Plan for Union County as extremely rural, with 60% being State Forest Land with a rural aesthetic character. The earliest records state that it was more than 78% forest with 75% mountainous terrain. The soils have developmental limitations due to low depth of bedrock and a high water table.

Hartley Township is the largest township in the county. It is bounded on the north by Centre County, on the east by Lewis Township (Union County), on the south by Snyder County, and on the west by Mifflin, and Centre Counties. The "Tight End" refers to the location near the intersection of Union, Centre, and Mifflin Counties where Penns Creek flows through an ever narrowing valley between White and Paddy Mountains. Pardee, now just a small neighborhood of homes and cabins, adjoins lands of Weikert residents directly to the east. During the height of the timbering boom, Pardee was a thriving community with two stores, a tavern and a post office. Many Weikert residents walked the short distance to work for the lumbering companies.

In 1891, E. V. d'Invillier's report to the State Board of Commissioners on the 2nd Geological Survey of Pennsylvania stated that Union County's southwest-to-northeast ridges are part of the 1500 mile Appalachian chain. Over time, Penns Creek and its branches eroded, exposing white Medina sandstone in White Mountain and ore sandstone folds over Paddy's Mountain.

Near the end of the nineteenth century, James Pursley opened ore-pits south of the Hironimus Church and just north of Penns Creek showing Clinton yellow shales. D. C. Johnson's mine (the old Zimmerman Mine), about 1½ miles below Cherry Run, yielded hard fossil ore. Other long forgotten mine names were Pursley's Perforated Hill Mine, the Libby and Sholter, the Lincoln, and the Galer and Aumiller Mines.

The area is fed by numerous springs as well as Penns Creek and its two major tributaries, Cherry Run and Weikert Run. At least eight minor runs feed Penns Creek in this area.

One county road, the east-west Weikert Road, is the only road through the village of Weikert and ends at the state forest road, Cherry Run Road, which extends northward 7½ miles to Pennsylvania State Route 45, Woodward, and Centre County. A southbound White Mountain Road crosses the Penns Creek Bridge and terminates less than one mile into Pennsylvania State forest roads. A few unpaved lanes, such as Jolly's Grove Lane and Little Mountain Lane, lead into small clusters of homes and cabins. Private dirt drives pass through woods and fields leading to single or just a few properties. The Weikert Road is maintained for winter travel, but sometimes only 4-wheel drive vehicles can be driven safely on the other roads and lanes.

Most properties did not have specific addresses until the 9/11 crisis, when the law mandated the naming of roads and the assigning of numerical addresses. Land owners chose the names for their drives or lanes. MAG Way is an example, where MAG represents the owner's initials. Others simply have lane numbers such as Lane 41.

In my opinion, it is with few exceptions, that the underlying strengths in families came through the matrilineal generations. Women were the "keepers of cleanliness, sobriety, manners, morals and decorum," as expressed by Mildred Armstrong Kalish in *Little Heathens* (Bantam, 2007).

Weikert women, as well as almost all country women, were the original multi-taskers. In the early settler years, families had to be almost totally self-sufficient. Some continued this way for many years. Children, too, had responsibilities and shared in most farm and home chores.

As with many women of these eras, Weikert women took care of babies, raised the children, and cared for the aged and ill relatives. Women planted and tended their own gardens and harvested and canned the fruits and vegetables. They raised and then preserved the meat from their cows, chickens and hogs. They prepared fish and eels from Penns Creek, Cherry Run and Weikert Run. It was the women and children who gathered berries, mushrooms, nuts and herbs. Families ate local rabbits, squirrels, ducks and pheasants.

It was mainly the women who learned how to prepare meats—venison, bear and wildfowl—that their family members hunted for on Jack's and Paddy's Mountains. They made their own bread, cakes, cookies, and pies. In that period, for much of the time the only things that money was spent on for the table were salt, sugar, tea, coffee, and white flour. Frequently butter and eggs were traded to get these necessities.

At a "Cracker Barrel Conversations" program in September of 2007, Harvey Boop related that his family's land was so barren that they lived on the meat from the mountains and the fish and eels from the creek. Guns were a part of everyday life, and women, as well as men, learned to shoot for self-protection, safety and security, and a means for providing food for the table. As families prospered somewhat, they aspired to own three guns—a .22 rifle, and ten and twelve gauge shotguns. In the twentieth century, every young boy dreamed of owning at least a BB gun.

It was the women who knitted or sewed their family's garments. They made quilts and knotted haps (stuffed comforters) for their beds. Often socks were darned many times over and clothes were cut down to smaller sizes as parts wore out. The motto in these homes could well have been "Use up, make do, do without."

Many early residents were born, raised, married, died and were buried within a small radius of Weikert. And finally, even though lives were already hard for the early settlers, the late 1920s and 1930s of the Great Depression made difficult lives even harder. Women survived great hardships with dignity.

In reprints in the 1994 edition of *Union County Heritage*, the 1796 excerpts from the West Buffalo Township census, which included Hartley Township, showed one hundred and ninety-two men and just two women who were listed as housekeepers. (Really? 192 men—and 2 women?) When Hartley Township became a separate township in

1811, there were one hundred and eighty men and, again, just two women listed. Historian Mary Belle Lontz has the 1815 assessment records for Hartley Township showing two hundred and thirteen men and seven women.

In contrast, in 2016 the Weikert population was one hundred and seventy people. The Federal Census in 2010 showed that the count was one hundred and forty one residents—seventy-eight were males and sixty-three were females.

In the beginning days of Hartley Township, many nowadays familiar names could be found there: Boop, Catherman, Cherry, Dorman, Green, Hendricks, Keister, Kleckner, Weikel, Weiker, and Zimmerman. By the 1830s and 1840s, the Johnsons, Sholters and Pursleys, as well as the Goodlanders, had arrived. Thomas McCurdy of Cherry Run gave an interview December 9, 1875, to C. E. Haus of the Mifflinburg Telegraph stating that he had moved to Cherry Run in 1836.

Abbott Green, a son of Revolutionary War General Joseph Green, lived on the south side of Penns Creek, close to the mouth of Weikert Run where he had a sawmill. He died in 1802 and the mill was still shown in 1807. Henry Hendricks ended his days in the "Tight End." Jesse Hendricks lived on the south side of the creek a short distance east of Cherry Run and also had a saw mill there. The Hendricks all lived at the upper (west) end of the valley and were said to be lumbermen and rafts men.

The Zimmerman family owned the land known as "Deep Hollow" slightly east of Weikert from the mountain to the creek. In 1814, John Kehler, now Galer, eventually a large land owner, was assessed as a tenant on the "Frenchman's Tract" (lands of Casper Cenas of Philadelphia). That area is more recently known as Lindale.

These early settlers built log cabins, acquired and cleared farmland, built structures to hold their animals, and as soon as they could, purchased parts of the nearby woodlands. George Weiker, who came from the Carlisle-York section of Pennsylvania in the 1820s, lived at the place that was afterwards known as "Goodlanders" in the "Tight End." Jacob Weiker, George's brother, lived on the south side of Penns Creek at the saw mill formerly owned by Joseph Green. The Weikers, as well as members of several other families, moved west to Ohio and Missouri.

Scant information exists about the place of religion in the lives of the very earliest inhabitants. It is known that in the "West End" there was an early Dunkard (akin to the River Brethren) church on the Keister property just east of Weikert on the Weikert Road. A few families buried their relatives in the Dunkard Cemetery also known as Keister's across the road from that church. A limited number of these settlers traveled a considerable distance to churches in Laurelton and Lincoln Chapel, some (such as John Sholter) even walking barefoot to save their shoes until they got to church when they put their shoes on.

In most Union County histories, only one or two sentences address religious activity in Weikert prior to the establishment of the Hironimus Church in 1888. Those remarks state that services were held in the school house prior to the erecting of the church building. That statement must refer to the Lindale School as the Hironimus School was completed after the church.

Even though Barnet women's names are on deeds and Lucinda Burns Hironimus owned property along with her husband Andrew, only Barnet men and Andrew ever received credit in print as donors of land and materials to establish the church. Early records are available for the Hironimus Church only as part of the White Springs

United Methodist charge. It must be recognized, however, that after 1888 many references to the events in the religious life of Weikert residents must surely be documenting activities that occurred in the Hironimus Church. It is currently impossible to distinguish the Hironimus services from others in the White Springs Circuit records (Gerri L. Aitkin).

Supposedly, many later Hironimus Church records were lost during a flood when they were stored in the home of a parishioner. Some scattered records tell of Sunday school teachers, attendees, and the leadership. Others refer to the Christian Endeavor Sunday School class and a few references were made to women serving as organists. Pastors from various denominations, both lay and professional clergymen, served the little Weikert church through the years.

The church provided a venue for socialization that the women did not have heretofore. It was acceptable for men to gather at stores, the post office, barns, and farm sales, but those places were not approved gathering places for women. In the early days of the church, men sat on one side of the church and the women of the congregation sat on the opposite side. When the William Valentines moved into the area, Carrie Snyder Valentine broke the barrier and sat next to her husband William for church services. The congregation never returned to the split seating arrangements.

Some families were deeply religious, reading their Bibles every day, with strong ties to the church for many generations, continuing until today. For others, little evidence remains of their participation. The Hironimus Church became independent and self-sufficient in 1998.

In 1899 and 1900, the well-known and respected early Union County historian Richard Van Boskirk Lincoln published a "History of Union County" in the *Mifflinburg Telegraph*. He said of the schools of Hartley Township: "It is the same old story of subscription schools in log huts with slab benches, the teachers being good, poor and indifferent, the first kind being the exception."

Shortly after 1795, east of Weikert, an early schoolhouse known as "the Keister School" was built on land of, and provided for by the will of, the late George Keister. About 1832, the log schoolhouse was followed by a subscription-supported frame building painted white and forever known as "the White School." The first teacher was said to be a good teacher but immoderately fond of firewater. Later this school was abandoned and sold.

The Pennsylvania School Act of 1836 amended and consolidated several previous educational Acts. It required that so-called "non-accepting" school districts should vote annually upon the question of schools or no schools. In the early years of the settlement, Hartley Township like many other rural areas simply voted "no" each year to providing schools, until the Pennsylvania State law required that free schools be provided. Historians such as Charles Loy Sanders and Charles M. "Cool" Snyder generally omitted reference to education in the Weikert area before the Lindale School, "the Red School," was opened.

In 1842, G. & H. Roush were awarded the contract for $188.00 to build a school at Lindale west of Weikert and east of Cherry Run. A United States Geological Survey marker is located on the front lawn of the property just a few feet from the Weikert Road. Once the Hironimus School was built and opened in 1898 on the west end of the property adjacent to the Hironimus Cemetery and Hironimus Union Church, the Lindale School was closed. Abandoned, the building then served many years as a hunting camp. Again R. V. B. Lincoln noted, "In 1829, there were 12 distilleries in Hartley

Township and 3 schools. By 1843, there were 12 schools and 3 distilleries."

Following additional school consolidations, the Hironimus School was closed and the Weikert children were transported to Laurelton for the early grades and to Mifflinburg for upper grades. Five closed school buildings were moved to Laurelton and made into the Hartley Township Community Center.

Until the 1900s, very few students continued their education beyond the first eight grades. Those who did so walked or rode the L. & T. train to the high school in Laurelton. Leona Sholter Wirt spoke in her oral history interviews about having to leave school an hour early to walk a mile to the Laurelton L. & T. railroad station to get a ride on the westbound train back to Weikert. Occasionally, kind draymen or wagoneers gave the children rides part of the way.

School buildings provided places for socialization for whole families in addition to education. One or two children of younger than school age occasionally followed their older siblings to school and usually were allowed to stay. One young student "dressed" her little brother up and took him to school for picture day—although if one looks at a school picture of a class from the Hironimus School, one can see that the children did not have much in the way of a wardrobe to dress "up" in.

Early census records sometimes showed that certain adults could not read or write. One of the Mrs. Johnsons spoke only Pennsylvania Dutch (German). Her husband spoke only English. Life at home must have been very interesting.

Occasionally names of teachers were publicized when they were hired by the school board, when they attended "institutes," or if school reorganizations occurred. Salaries also were usually published. Unfortunately, there is no continuity of records. In the earliest days, many teachers had simply completed their high school studies just a year or two ahead of their students. These teachers attended courses at state normal schools to further their own education and to achieve certification.

Again, in the earliest days, teachers tended to be men. School board rules of conduct stood in the way of women. Women teachers were not allowed to be seen in bars or taverns, get their haircut in a commercial salon, or marry. Teachers' salaries were very low. Frequently they had to provide supplies, arrive early, carry in wood, start the fire in the stove, and get water at a nearby spring or neighboring farm pump. All of this in addition to teaching all eight grades of children. Often older children in the upper grades assisted with teaching the younger classes.

Some local teachers were Sherwood Libby, Martha Jean Krick (Yocum), Ida Libby (Barnett) for a summer term, Mary Etta Ely Johnson, and David Johnson. After 1920, a number of local Weikert women taught skills at the Laurelton State Village. For most residents, it was very simple basic studies interspersed with hands-on occupational training.

In the nineteenth century medical care outside the home was almost non-existent. Families did their own doctoring with home remedies and herbs, often using a wide variety of wild plants for medicinal teas. Early care, before there were doctors in Laurelton, was occasionally provided by mid-wives and pow-wowers. Lydia Boop, Mrs. Dorman, and Phoebe Styers were said to be pow-wow practitioners.

Infants died from whooping cough, diphtheria, croup, and pneumonia, if they survived at birth. Women died from tuberculosis and during childbirth, and men frequently died from work-related accidents at the lumbering companies, on the railroad, and in farming. Once the railroad was available, very ill or injured residents were placed upon the east-bound Lewisburg-Tyrone trains in hopes that they would survive the trip to the hospital in Sunbury. Sadly, they frequently did not. "No wonder drugs or medical miracles meant suffering and early death. Chronic pain and sickroom stench—witnessed, handled, felt—drained every life, especially women's"—as chronicled by Douglas Macneal in *Centre County Heritage* (vol. 38, 2003).

In the very early twentieth century when the State of Pennsylvania mandated that death certificates must be filed stating the cause of death, of 43 death certificates filed for this area, only two stated that cancer was the cause of death. To have cancer in the family was a stigma, so other terms were used, such as dropsy, apoplexy, and disease of the heart. Shortly after the State required the doctors to file death certificates, a list of correct spellings of diseases was provided in order that filers might list causes of death more accurately. For 29 of the women subjects for whom death certificates were obtainable and covered the years from 1911 to 1964, there were still no certificates filed with cancer as the diagnosis. Coronary conditions were the prime causes of death listed.

Some tuberculosis patients were sent to the state sanatoriums at Hamburg and Danville. Again, most did not return home. Patients with mental health problems were sent to the Danville State Hospital. Very occasionally, after 1920 when the Laurelton State Institution for Feeble-Minded Women of Child-Bearing Age had opened, a local woman might be placed there for care.

In a recent lecture for the Union County Historical Society, Kate Hastings, a rural sociologist at Susquehanna University, said that from 1906 until 1963 tuberculosis was the third leading cause of death in Pennsylvania. In 1910, 27% of deaths were in people under the age of five years. As late as 1911, a female born that year had a life expectancy of fifty-four years according to an article in the *Millmont Times*, December 1, 2011.

Flu epidemics were the most virulent. The epidemic of 1917–18 wiped out whole households. Local doctors, particularly Doctor Glover of Laurelton, worked round the clock frequently to the detriment of their own health. Ruth Ann Wilson Bilger's elderly father from Huntingdon County traveled to Union County to help with the critically ill members of the household.

Many children were sent to school in the winter wearing Asphidity bags of smelly herbs around their necks to ward off colds and other illnesses. Mustard plasters and peroxide were used to treat various conditions. Home medical remedies were almost equally balanced by superstitions.

In the earliest years of settlement in the West End, meeting life's basic needs and simply surviving filled the time of both women and men. In the isolated very rural areas, during the first half of the nineteenth century, frequently poor families had little choice but to socialize within their extended family and other settlers living relatively nearby.

Eventually, family reunions and church and lodge picnics became available to all but the most isolated and impoverished families. Picnics were a major part of summer activities, whether large community events or simple family gatherings. Of course, the women prepared all of the food—the standard daily foods with a few specialty items. After completing many hours of oral history interviews asking about picnics, Louise Goehring Scott felt that there were more pickled beets per person in Union County than anywhere else.

Once schools and churches were built in the later decades of the 1800s, more venues for social interaction became available for women and families. Women's chief pleasures were their families, church activities, Sunday school, dinners, and community festivals. A special thrill for Weikert residents—especially the children—were the occasions when Allen Jolly would set up his horse-drawn carousel, "The Flying Jenny," in downtown Weikert.

Weikert was known for its excellent fiddlers, particularly the Barnet men. Barn dances were often held in the Shaffer barn at Lindale. At first these "dances" or gatherings were attended by men only. As the nineteenth century drew to a close, women began to attend. Until the 1920s and the participation of women visitors in the cabins and camps, the well-known Weikert peach brandy was shunned by the Weikert women residents.

After the L. & T. railroad arrived, people could travel to larger towns for excursions, the occasional oyster suppers, amusement parks, or county fairs such as the Centre County Grange Encampment. It was at these events that young women and men met other folks from outside of Weikert, often resulting in marriages.

Both women and men enjoyed day trips that became a three-times-a-year excursions into the woods. The Laurelton Lumber Company would take people up on the mountains on their lumber trains pulled by the dinky engines. In the spring the attendees would gather arbutus for fragrance; in the summer they picked huckleberries; and in the fall they gathered chestnuts.

Sometimes the best remembered and appreciated amusements were "singings," musical evenings held at home, or Mary Blanche Bracken Jolly's taffy pulls for her daughters, Hilda and Isabelle, and their young women friends. Later, in the mid-twentieth century, both men and women enjoyed "home movies" that were brought by campers and fishermen to be shown at the Weikert Store.

There were definite differences and distinctions in the lives of Weikert women and Weikert men. Men could be in local fiddler or community bands and could go alone to barn dances, out of town events, or even out of the area, particularly if they were fiddlers. "Jake" Barnett had several bands. Men played on baseball teams that traveled to other communities. Men went off for weeks at a time to hunting and fishing camps leaving the women at home to manage the household, tend the animals and gardens, care for the children and aging relatives, and sometimes keep the store. Men could congregate in stores, railroad shanties, post offices, and each other's barns.

Some men who were small business owners went "to town" on the train for business purposes, kept much of the money they earned, and were known by their own first names. Women were known as "Mrs." A young girl raised in the center of Weikert wondered why women didn't have first names. Her neighbor was known as "Sime", short for his first name Simon, and his wife was known as "Mrs. Sime." In later years, men had cars and definitely were the ones to do the driving. Two early automobiles in Weikert belonged to John C. Krumrine and Dave Libby.

Women seldom had the opportunity to enjoy pleasures outside of the home. The old German saying of "Kinder, Kuche and Kirche"—children, cooking and church—still held true until the beginning of World War II. There were a limited number of quilting bees, Bible-reading prayer groups, and needlework and craft groups. Two general sayings of the day gave an indication of the status of women: "Whistling girls and crowing hens always come to some bad end," and, "Women and children should be seen and not heard." Of course, the women may have quietly been thinking, "The rooster crows but the hen delivers the goods."

Until approximately the 1920s, few women had opportunities to earn any money for themselves. A very limited number of women were able to become postmasters when their fathers, uncles or husbands gave up the position. A few women ran boarding houses for single workmen, fishermen, and summer vacationers. An occasional woman was "involved in business of the less than approved sort." Leona Sholter Wirt said that these women lived in Pardee, where they could do things that they couldn't get away with in Weikert. Not all of this occurred just in Pardee.

Until World War II era, women didn't smoke, drink or swear in public. Some "wild goings on" did occur among visitors to hunting and fishing camps, but not by resident Weikert women. As mentioned, women school teachers could not keep their jobs if they entered a barroom, got their hair done at a "salon," or married. In Easton, Pennsylvania, even in the late 1940s, all of my elementary school teachers were maiden ladies with the exception of the principal, who was a married lady, but with no children.

It really was a man's world. An Irish Labor party statement was that "the men were slaves to the bosses (anyone in authority) and the women were slaves to the men." Sadly, that statement described much of early Weikert women's lives until the time of World War II.

Very little if anything is known as to the source of the money that the earliest settlers initially had for purchasing their lands. Six members of the Jacob Hironimus family came to America on the Brig "Osgood" in 1819, which was an expensive trip. The Barnets moved to the area from Bucks County, Pennsylvania, and may have sold property there in order to purchase their Weikert lands. For others the finances are simply unknown. At the time, sketchy histories do not refer to any families as prosperous.

After the original settlers, some people were able to acquire additional lands. Many became "land poor." They were people who owned a lot of land, but had very little money to pay the taxes. The first William Johnson at one time owned 18,000 acres of the far "West End." Parts of these holdings were bought, sold, or lost for taxes in many of the later years of Johnson's life. Money to "pay the taxes" was, and still is for some farmers, the biggest financial concern of their lives.

Sayings in use at the time give an indication of the lack of money. They would drink "Adam's Ale"—a glass of water—or go by "Shank's Mare"—meaning to go by foot—and the self-explanatory, "Waste not, want not." The life and times of the nineteenth century would be viewed by modern day observers as "hard times." Weikert life was so isolated from the commerce of the outside world that the Panic of 1857 and the following depression did not warrant a line in any Union County history for the West End.

As enough products could be grown or obtained by hunting and especially fishing to meet a family's own needs, it became possible to sell wheat, corn, and hay that could be shipped during high water on rafts down Penns Creek to Sunbury and beyond. It eventually became more productive to convert the grains to whiskey and to ship the product that way. Fish and eels were sold locally or to a huckster who came around. Prior to the railroad, wood was shipped out by wagon loads.

Men could occasionally earn extra money as day laborers for others. The county paid a scalp bounty between 25 cents and $2.00 for fox, mink, weasel, wildcat, polecats and hawks deemed unwelcome varmints. Women could trade extra eggs and butter at the store for necessities such as sugar, coffee, salt and white flour.

The Industrial Revolution of the nineteenth century came to the Weikert area later than in many other places, but did bring the railroads, timbering, and relatively small mines and foundries. For many years after its completion to Bellefonte in 1887, the L. & T. Railroad was Weikert's link to the outside world. The lack of a through road had kept Weikert an isolated pocket. The railroad provided the means for small timber operators as well as major lumber companies to ship their goods. Wood cut in the West End was not of the highest quality. It was shipped as "pitch pine and prop timber" to the Pennsylvania coal regions as told by Benjamin F. G. Kline, Jr., in his 1971 book of that name. Timber income and wages disappeared by 1900 when the timber industry collapsed for the West End.

In *Silhouettes* (1985), Lois Kalp of Lewisburg wrote, "It is difficult for women today to understand the chattel-like condition of women in 1914 [...]. Women had no political rights. Unmarried women were better off than married women in matters of property and personal rights. A wife could not sell and convey real estate unless her husband joined on the deed; he however could do so without his wife's consent [...]. A wife's fixed interest in her husband's estate was called a 'dower'; the husband's in his wife's estate was called a 'curtesy', the latter being more valuable. The wife's interest was one-third of her husband's estate; her husband's 'curtesy' was on all of his wife's estate."

According to the Pennsylvania State Archives of Historical Museum Documents, the Public Law 35 of 1872 gave women the right to retain money they had earned. In Bradford County in court cases of 1873–1891 and Erie County 1875–1887 married women still had to sue to get their separate earnings. Is it any wonder that this thought was often expressed by "old maids" now politically correctly called "single women"—"I have a dog that growls, a chimney that smokes, a parrot that swears and a cat that stays out all night. Why do I need a husband?"

For the lucky women and men of the area who were able to obtain employment there, the opening in 1917 of the Laurelton State Village for Feeble-Minded Women of Child-Bearing Age served somewhat as a buffer to the Great Depression. In the late 1920s and the 1930s, the Depression, for many, meant the ever-looming threat of going from poverty to destitution. Money, jobs, farms, livestock, machinery and people's small savings disappeared.

With the exception of the establishment of the CCC Camps, Roosevelt's New Deal and Poverty Plans of the 1930s and 1940s never reached the people of Weikert. With World War II there was a major shift of employment out of the area, and young men left to go to war. Following the war, many of these young men took their newly acquired skill elsewhere. The population of Weikert no longer expanded, with the exception of recreational part-time residents.

In the spring of 2016, I attended an excellent Power Point program by Jonathan Bastian, Pardee historian, about the men of Pardee and the lumbering operations there. I came to realize that while men were mentioned in many forms of history, the women of the West End, more specifically the "Tight End" of Union County, were given little if any notice at all. I decided to try and tell some of their story.

While my previous books about the Weikert area focused on the properties or the cabins and camps, this book is a compilation of the known statistical information about these women, some family members' memories, their pictures when I was able to locate them, and sadly, last but not least, pictures of their tombstones which somewhat give recognition to the fact that they did exist.

When my interest in Weikert began forty-two years ago, during a camping trip with my children to the Cherry Run area in 1975, I never dreamed I would be interested in compiling information for others. I listened carefully to stories I was told, but did not document the details. I did begin collecting small histories, deeds, some pictures, and much family and folklore along the way, now amounting to twenty-five notebooks of information. My regret is that during those very hectic days of my earlier life, I could not do more to interview these wonderful women and to get more of their stories. Beginning in 1980, when I was a full-time cabin resident for a year, in the following years, when I was the house-sitter for friends at "Avian Haven," the Snooks, "Jolly's Grove," the Barnets, and "Serendipity" at Cherry Run, the Johnsons, and even to the present day, friends loved to tell stories. Betty and Harry Snook, Leona Sholter Wirt, Genevieve Weaser, Ed Barnet, Nick Nash and Jerry Sholter shared their recollections. Judy Shively Wagner, J. Helen Bauer, Tony Shively in the Millmont Times, August "Pop" Barnett, and now Micalee Sullivan in the West End Quarterly, have managed to record and save valuable memories and history.

Frequently, when I would return to "Serenity," our cabin at Little Mountain, from an event in the "Tight End" area and relate a story to Dean Jansma, both before and after our marriage, he would ask if that story was from the Post Office, the Store, or just general Weikert rumor. Often it was difficult to get a full story from any source, and there are still tales out there to be uncovered. Henry Shoemaker, Pennsylvania's first State Folklorist, did stay in Weikert for a time, with the Ace Sholter family. Henry took small wisps of wild animal stories and embellished them to add excitement. Once I was able to get people to talk about their experiences, I found no need to embellish the stories.

Women of Weikert

circa 1820–2012

Women of Weikert, circa 1820–2012

BARBARA ALBRIGHT
    MRS. JESSE HENDRICKS
dau. of Frederick Albright
mar. Jesse Hendricks

Lived on south side of Penns Creek, a short distance east of Cherry Run. On July 9, 1817, in Union County Deed Book (C-407), she signed on to appoint an attorney for the F. Albright estate. By 1826 Jesse was living on H. Roush land. By 1831 he was taxed on 210 acres.

By 1841 debt was levied against Jesse. He had 200 acres or more—six acres of land with a two-story log house, a sawmill, an apple press, a number of fruit trees, and several springs—Union County Deed Book P, pp. 329–30. By the 1850 census Jesse, 62, a laborer, had a wife Mary, 51. In the 1856 Iowa State Census for Cox Creek, Clayton Co, Iowa, Jesse, 66, was a farmer, and wife Mary, 55.

MARIA "MARY" (WEIKER)
    MRS. GEORGE WEIKER
b. around 1770
d. Dec. 12, 1849 or 1853
bur. Moreland Cemetery, Wayne Co, Ohio
mar. George Weiker

He was a gunsmith in Bucks Co, moved to Union Co around 1800. He is listed in a Hartley Township assessment record as Wiker. They left for Ohio before 1840, selling land to Benjamin Goodlander.

Children: George Jr., Samuel, Adam, Peter, and an unnamed child.

CATHARINA WEIKER
    MRS. JACOB BARNET
bur. Hironimus Union Church Cemetery, Weikert, Union Co, PA
dau. of George Weiker Sr. and Magdalena Maria Reinarin Weiker
mar. Jacob Barnet (Bernt) around 1800
They owned a farm in 1793.

Children: John Barnet (*b.* around 1800)

Mary Deal or Diehl
    Mrs. Jacob Weiker
b. 1774, Bucks Co, PA
d. Aug. 4, 1849
bur. Lowell School Cemetery, Seneca Co, Ohio
dau. of Frederick Diehl and Susanna Spinner Diehl
mar. Jacob Weiker, April 7, 1795

Probably from Bucks County, he moved to Union County in 1800. In 1815 a Hartley Township assessment record listed him as Wilker with a sawmill. Moved to Seneca County, Ohio, in 1834.

Children: Mahdelena, Elizabeth, Salome, Catarina, Joseph, Jacob, Susanna, Hannah, Anna.

[F.A.G. 62117275]

Barbara Clymer
    Mrs. Henry Hendricks
mar. Henry Hendricks

From Hendricks Book, Union County Historical Society. Lived at Cherry Run area. Her second son was Jesse Hendricks.

Eve (Eva, Eave) Zeiter
    Mrs. Jacob Hironimus
b. Oct. 10, 1778, Uhrwiller, Alsace (Germany/France)
d. 1852, Union Co, PA
dau. of Johann Georg Zeiter and Margaretha Kiehl Zeiter
mar. Jacob Hironimus Sr., Feb. 5, 1795, Uhrwiller, Alsace

Came to the U.S. on the ship *Osgood* from Amsterdam and landed Sept. 20, 1819. In 1820 census resided in Hartleton, Hartley Twsp. In 1850 census House 138 with Jacob Sr., Mary, Jacob Jr. and his wife Hannah.

Children: Catherine (*b.* 1798, *mar.* Adam Ackerman), Mary (*b.* 1800, in Germany), Jacob Jr. (*b.* 1804), Margaretha (*mar.* Christian Sheffer or Shaffer), Eva (*b.* 1809, *d.* 1877? *mar.* John Barnet).

Hannah Burd or Barnd
    Mrs. Jacob Hironimus
b. around 1799, Bucks Co, PA
d. 1860, Union Co, PA
mar. Jacob Hironimus Jr., Oct. 27, 1831, Mifflinburg, Union Co, PA

Her maiden name Barnd in Rev. John George Anspach's record of 1831. In 1850 census House 138, he was 46, she was 51, John, 18, Catherine, 11, William, 8. Also in household, Jacob Hironimus Sr., 73, his wife Eave (Eve), 71, their daughter Mary, 50.

Children: John (*mar.* Elizabeth and moved west), Catherine (Kathryn, had children Hattie and Calvin Catherman), William (*mar.* Nancy Hassinger), Andrew (*b.* 1837, *mar.* Lucinda Burns).

ANNA MARIA "MARY" HIRONIMUS
b. March 21, 1800, in Alsace, France
dau. of Jacob Hironimus Sr. and Eave (Eve) Zeiter Hironimus.

She arrived in the U.S. with her parents and siblings on Sept. 20, 1819, on the brig *Osgood*. In 1850 census House 138, with parents and brother's family.

CATHERINE HIRONIMUS
    MRS. ADAM ACKERMAN
b. Jan. 29, 1798; in 1850 census *b.* Germany, in 1860 census *b.* Alsace, France
d. Jan. 16, 1874, Union Co, PA
bur. Keister Cemetery, Union Co, PA
dau. of Jacob Hironimus Sr. and Eve Zeiter Hironimus
mar. Adam (or Adour?) Ackerman

Arrived in the U.S. around 1820 on the brig *Osgood*. Lived on the north side of the Weikert Road in the Lindale area. In 1850 census House 37, he was 52, she was 52, Andrew Hironimus, 8, living with them. In 1860 census, Lewis Shaffer, 17, and Daniel Moyer, 12, living with them.

[F.A.G. 13626471]

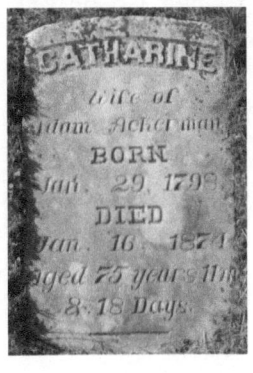

Catharine wife of
Adam Ackerman
(permission:
Bruce Fisher)

MARGARETHA HIRONIMUS
   MRS. CHRISTIAN SHAFFER
b. March 19, 1806, Uhrwiller, Alsace, France
d. June 10, 1879, Union Co, PA
bur. Ray's Church Cemetery (St. Peter's Church Cemetery), Union Co, PA
dau. of Jacob Hironimus and Eve Zeiter Hironimus
mar. Christian Shaffer, Feb. 4, 1834, West Buffalo Twsp, Union Co

She came to the United States in 1819 with her family. Grandmother of Ammon J. Shaffer.

Children: Mary, Jacob, Sebastian, Nancy, Lewis, Christian.
[F.A.G. 125546833]

Margaret wife of Christian Shaffer (permission: F.A.G.)

EVA "EAVE" HIRONIMUS
   MRS. JOHN BARNET
b. Oct. 22, 1807 or 1810, Alsace, France or Germany
d. Dec. 6, 1877
bur. Keister Cemetery, Hartley Township, Union Co, PA
dau. of Jacob Hironimus Sr. and Eve Zeiter Hironimus
mar. John Barnet

Arrived in U.S. about 1820. In 1850 census House 136. In 1860 census John was 50, Eve was 41.

Children (in 1850 census): Jacob F., 17, George O., 14, James, 11.
[F.A.G. 13697832]

Eva wife of John Barnet (permission: Leann Keefer Bechdel)

ELIZABETH (GALER, HENDRICKS)
    MRS. DANIEL GALER
    MRS. LAURENCE HENRY HENDRICKS
b. around 1816
mar. 1. Daniel Galer
mar. 2. Laurence Henry Hendricks, son of Abraham and Hannah Hendricks

In 1850 census Daniel was 31, she was 34, Andrew was 6, Margaret 6-12 months. Daniel, whose brothers Michael and John owned a sawmill, died in a hunting accident in 1852. In 1860 census Lawrence was 30, she was 45, Andrew was 16, Margaret 10, Mary Galer, 8, Nathaniel Hendricks 1. Hendricks land abutted Galer early on: Beers map of 1868 shows property on the south side of the Weikert Road between J. Galer and J. Hironimus. By 1869 they had moved to Glaze Twsp, Miller Co, Missouri, and had sold their land to Alanson Johnson.

Children: Andrew, Margaret and Mary Galer, Nathaniel Hendricks.

MARY ELIZABETH (GOODLANDER)
    MRS. BENJAMIN GOODLANDER
b. 1783, in PA
d. Oct. 7, 1880
bur. Lincoln Chapel Cemetery, Laurelton, Union Co, PA
mar. Benjamin Goodlander

In 1834 they began a church group that grew into Lincoln Chapel. In 1840 they are listed in Hartley Twsp. In 1850 census House 132. He was a farmer. Another list says he was a weaver. In the household were Martha Sholter and Mary Sholter, 16. In 1875, as widow of Benjamin, she sold one acre and 123 perches to the railroad for $50. In 1879 she granted land to the railroad. In 1880 she was living with her granddaughter Jamilla Winkel (Weikel?).

Children: Christopher (Christian), Martha (*mar.* William Moyer), Catherine (*mar.* John Sholter), John D.
[F.A.G. 75098506]

Mary E. wife of
B. Goodlander
(permission:
Karin Randall)

ELIZABETH WERTZ (WUERZ)
   MRS. CHRISTIAN GOODLANDER
b. 1766, in PA
bur. Lincoln Chapel Cemetery, Union Co, PA
dau. of Johann Dietrich Wuerz and Mary Barbara Strauss
mar. Christian Goodlander, June 17, 1787, Berks Co, PA.

CATHERINE or CATHARINA GOODLANDER
   MRS. JOHN E. SHOLTER
b. Nov. 1, 1810, Northumberland Co, PA
d. Feb. 20, 1884, Weikert, Union Co, PA
bur. Hironimus Union Church Cemetery, Weikert, Union Co, PA
dau. of Benjamin Goodlander and Mary Elizabeth (?) Goodlander
mar. John E. Sholter, Jan. 11, 1834

She was a sister of Benjamin Goodlander, a land purchaser in 1830–40. She was an ancestor of Newt Gingrich (Speaker, United States House of Representatives, 1995–9) via her daughter Catherine McPherson, the latter's son Newton, his daughter Louise, and her son Newton Searles McPherson. Catherine smoked a pipe. In 1850 census House 131, he was 44, she was 39, Mary, 16, Sarahann, 13, Henry, 12, Margaret, 9, Martha, 7, Harriet, 5,

Benjamin, 3. The 1860 census includes William, 6, and George, 4.

Children: Sarah Catherine (*b.* March 23, 1833, *d.* June 9, 1888), Mary Elizabeth (*b.* around 1835), Henry (*b.* April 19, 1837), Margaret R. (*b.* 1841), Martha Jane (*b.* 1843), Hannah M. (*b.* 1844, *d.* 1934, *mar.* Joseph L. Wallace), Benjamin Frank (*b.* April 21, 1850, Weikert, *d.* April 11, 1922), William C. (*b.* July 1853, *d.* 1937), George Washington (*b.* Aug. 1856, *d.* 1930).

[F.A.G. 29553440]

Catharine wife of John Sholter (permission: Bill Cunningham)

ELIZA GOODLANDER
MRS. JACOB SHIRK
b. May 18, 1813
d. Dec. 1, 1886
bur. Keister Cemetery, Union Co, PA
mar. Jacob Shirk (*b.* Lancaster Co, PA)

In 1850 census House 148, he was 45, she was 36.

Children (in 1850 census): Levina, 11, Susannah, 10, Eliz., 8, Abr., 6, Samuel, 4, Catherine, 2, Angeline.

[F.A.G. 10351198]

Elizabeth wife of Jacob Shirk (permission: Waterfall)

JANE E. (GOODLANDER)
    MRS. CHRISTOPHER GOODLANDER
b. around 1825
mar. Christopher Goodlander, *div.* Dec. 1870

In 1850 census House 130. He was a farmer.

Children (in 1850 census): Nancy, 7, Mary 4, Sarahann, 3 (*mar.* Zachary Galer).

SARAH HARTMAN
    MRS. GEORGE MICHAEL AUMILLER
b. May 19, 1825, or May 18, 1824, Catawissa, Columbia Co, PA
d. March 7, 1890, Union Co, PA
bur. Hironimus Union Church Cemetery, Weikert, Union Co, PA
dau. of William Hartman and Mary Hartman
mar. George Michael Aumiller Jr., Feb. 22, 1842, New Berlin (or Laurelton), Union Co, PA

He was a lumberman and a mine owner. She was from a family of circus performers. At Danville, PA, some died of typhoid fever, so the family bought a hotel and settled there.

Children: Michael William, Percival S., Annie, George Washington, Jeremiah, James, Crawford C., Manassah T., Lavina (*mar.* Carpenter), Hattie Mabel (*mar.* Renn), Mary Jane "Jennie" (*mar.* Rheppard).

[F.A.G. 74041924]

Sarah wife of
George Aumiller
(permission:
Bill Cunningham)

Women of Weikert

ELIZABETH "ELIZA" SWITZER
MRS. WILLIAM P. PURSLEY

b. April 12, 1817, Juniata Co, PA
d. Aug. 16 or 4, 1896, Weikert, Union Co, PA
bur. Hironimus Union Church Cemetery, Weikert, Union Co, PA
dau. of David Switzer and Elizabeth Switzer
mar. William Pursley

He was originally from Milroy, PA. By 1850 they were farming west of Weikert. In 1850 census House 147, he was 38, she was 30, Ann, 10, Mary, 8, James, 6, Marcus, 4, David, 2. In 1870 census Daniel, 21, Reed, 18, Joseph, 15, William B., 10. 1880 census mentions son Reed and grandson Oscar Reed Goodlander. At one time she was a member of White Springs UMC Circuit. She became a midwife in the village later in life. She died of dropsy of the heart.

Children: Ann, Mary, James C. (*b.* Oct. 3, 1844, *bap.* Nov. 9, 1879, White Springs UMC Circuit), Marcus, David or Daniel, Reed, Joseph, William B.

[F.A.G. 99956138]

Eliza wife of
Wm Pursley
(permission:
Bill Cunningham)

JANE SWITZER
MRS. JOHN GALER

b. Jan. 1822
d. April 15, 1886
bur. Hironimus Union Church Cemetery, Weikert, Union Co, PA
dau. of David Switzer and Elizabeth Switzer
mar. John Galer Jr., 1844

In 1850 census house 146, he was 40, she was 25, also Zaccariah; a John Romich is in the household. In 1874–6 they granted land leases to the railroad. In 1875 they sold with Mr. and Mrs. Zach Galer 1 acre 110 perches to the railroad for $322.50. A Jane Galer was listed on the White Springs Circuit Church roll.

Children: David C. Galer (*b.* 1857), John W., Mary A., Jacob C., Elizabeth (?), Catherine.

[F.A.G. 99956113]

Jane wife of
John Galer
(permission:
Bill Cunningham)

CATHARINE SWITZER
MRS. WILLIAM JOHNSON
b. around 1826
d. Feb. 9, 1883
bur. Hironimus Union Church Cemetery, Weikert, Union Co, PA
dau. of David Switzer and Elizabeth Switzer
mar. William Johnson, June 17, 1841, Mifflin Co, PA

She was originally from Milroy (before 1840) and spoke only Pennsylvania Dutch. In 1850 census House 145, he was 37, she was 25, William, 8, Anna, 5, Alaston (*sic*), 3, Auminda, 1. 1860 census also includes David C., 8.

Children: William (a farmer at Cherry Run, Hartley Tswp), Anna M. (*d.* 1876? *mar.* S. C. Wilt of Hartleton), Alanson (lived in Laurelton), Armanda or Orminda (*mar.* David Benney), David C. (lived in Hartley Twsp), Mary (*d.* at age 3), Catherine Gertrude (*d.* at age 13).

[F.A.G. 63546796]

Women of Weikert 33

Johnson
Catharine
(permission:
Bill Cunningham)

Mrs. Jacob Berkstressor
d. probably before 1850 census
mar. Jacob Berkstressor (*b.* around 1800)
 In 1850 census House 144. Jacob Berkstressors may have moved to Kentucky.
 Children (in 1850 census): Phoebe, 20, Stewart, 18, Edwin, 16, Margaret, 8, Joseph, 5.

Hannah (Hendricks)
 Mrs. Abraham Hendricks
mar. Abraham Hendricks
 In 1850 census House 142, he was 64, she was 50, Lawrence, 24.

Ann Overt
b. around 1782, New Jersey
 In 1850 census living in the home of John and Margaret Goodlander, household 129.

Hannah (Hartman)
 Mrs. John Hartman
b. Sept. 12, 1786, in Maryland
d. Aug. 20, 1864 or 1860
bur. Keister Cemetery, Hartley Twsp, Union Co, PA
mar. John Hartman
 In 1850 census House 140, he was 71, she was 65; Frederick Bingaman, 14, in household. They were between John Gailor and Thomas McCurdy

near Cherry Run. The 1860 census says that she was born in Maryland.
[F.A.G. 13626238]

Hannah wife of
J. Hartman
(Leann Keefer
Bechdel)

MARY (MILLER)
   MRS. PETER MILLER
b. May 21, 1786
d. Oct. 4, 1872
bur. Keister Cemetery, Weikert, Union Co, PA
mar. Peter Miller

In 1850 census House 149, he was 65, she was 63; son Andrew, 30, wife Hannah, 28, Rachal, 10, Rebecca, 8, Jacob, 6. In 1860 not in Weikert.
   [F.A.G. 122015727]

Mary wife of
Peter Miller
(permission:
F.A.G.)

Susan (McCurdy)
Mrs. Thomas McCurdy
b. around 1799
d. before 1880
mar. Thomas McCurdy

Thomas McCurdy (McCandy in 1850, McCurley in 1860, Curdy at burial) came from Mifflinburg. They lived on the John Donlop Warrant of 1794, 1.75 acres from Cherry Run to private lane along the Weikert Road. In 1850 census House 141, he was 53, she was 51, Mary, 20, Forster, 18, Samuel, 14, Thomas, 9. In 1875 they sold three acres and 26 perches to the railroad for $190.50 and a further 1 acre and 50 perches for $83.75.

Children (in 1860 census): Mary, 28, Foster (Forster), 26, Samuel, 24, Thomas, 19.

Catharine Shively
Mrs. Henry Keister
Mrs. Samuel Keister
Mrs. William Bohnestiehl
b. Aug. 10, 1803
d. Jan. 29, 1873
bur. Keister Cemetery, Hartley Twsp, Union Co, PA (as Bonestell)
dau. of John Shively and Elizabeth Dersham Shively
mar. 1. Henry Keister
mar. 2. his son Samuel Keister
mar. 3. William Bohnestiel (Bonestell)

In 1850 census House 135, Bonasteel. He was 48, she was 46. In 1860 census Jacob Barlet (Barnet), 28, a laborer, lived with them. In 1875 they sold 132 perches to the railroad for $140.

[F.A.G. 13697888]

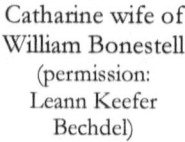

Catharine wife of
William Bonestell
(permission:
Leann Keefer
Bechdel)

ANN JANE "ANNIE" PURSLEY
  MRS. THOMAS LIBBY
b. June 27, 1840? Laurelton, Union Co, PA
d. July 14, 1911, Pardee Station, Union Co, PA
bur. Hironimus Union Church Cemetery, Weikert, Union Co, PA
dau. of William Pursley and Eliza Switzer Pursley
mar. Thomas Libby, 1857, Laurelton, Union Co, PA, his second wife

He came to Union Co in 1852. In 1875 they sold two acres and 92 perches to the railroad for $22.50. In 1900 census House 26, he was 74, she was 59. She is listed on the White Springs UMC Circuit Membership Roll. She was a kind and devoted mother.

Children: Albert, William, John, Daniel Cary, Thomas, Asa (*b.* Nov. 19, 1866), Samuel, David (*b.* Jan. 1, 1869, *mar.* Emma Jane McPherson), Mary Ellen (*b.* Dec. 7, 1875), Charles (*b.* Aug. 7, 1878). Asa, David, Mary Ellen and Charles were *bap.* Dec. 8, 1879, White Springs UMC Circuit.

[F.A.G. 91836703]

(permission:
Wirt/Boop)

Women of Weikert

MARY (BOOB)
MRS. MICHAEL BOOB
b. around 1806
mar. Michael Boob

In 1850 census House 134, he was 45, she was 44, Elizabeth, 20, Sarah, 19, Lydia, 17, Catherine, 16, William, 14, Julian, 12, Daniel, 10. They lived between Daniel Gahler, House 133, and William Bohnestiehl, House 135. In 1860 census, not in Weikert.

Children: Elizabeth, Sarah, Lydia, Catherine, William, Julian, Daniel, John, James, Samuel, Margaret.

MARGARET (GOODLANDER)
MRS. JOHN D. GOODLANDER
b. Feb. 23, 1810
d. Dec. 8, 1874
bur. Lincoln Chapel Cemetery, Laurelton, Union Co, PA
mar. John D. Goodlander

In 1850 census House 129; Ann Overt or Cavant, 68 (*b.* New Jersey) was living in the household. In 1860 census only John L. is living with them; they are not in Weikert. In 1874 he granted a lease to the railroad.

Children (in 1850 census): Maryann, 11, John L. C., 10, Maria Sarah, 8.
[F.A.G. 22584203]

Margaret Goodlander
(permission: Karin Randall)

ELIZABETH (KALER)
　MRS. MICHAEL KALER
b. around 1814
mar. Michael Kaler (Galer?)

In 1850 census House 139, he was 35, she was 36. In the household were David Romick, 12, and Catherine, 16.

Children (in 1850 census): Mary, 7, Hannah, 2.

MARY (HUNTER)
　MRS. CHARLES J. HUNTER
b. around 1820
bur. Keister Cemetery, Hartley Twsp, Union Co, PA
mar. Charles J. Hunter (*b.* 1821, *d.* 1861)

In 1850 census House 143, he was 28, she was 30. In 1860 census no longer in Weikert.

Children (in 1850 census): Sarah J., 6, Franklin, 5, Joseph H. (died at age 6 in 1854), 2.

SARA(H) ANN PENNINGTON or SCRIBNER
　MRS. ALVAH MARSTON
b. March 20, 1814, Maine
d. Feb. 17, 1879
bur. Keister Cemetery, Weikert, Union Co, PA
mar. Alvah Marston Sr.

Moved to Weikert in 1850s. Alvah managed the Scribner & Perkins Lumber Company. In 1860 census he was 51, she was 46.

Children: James (*b.* in Maine), 21, Vesta (*b.* in Maine), 19, Alvah (*b.* Feb. 8, 1843, in Maine), 17, Charles (*b.* in Maine), 5, Adda (*b.* in PA), 2. Alvah and Charles *bap.* Nov. 9, 1879, White Springs UMC Circuit.

[F.A.G. 86894520]

Sarah A. wife of
Alvah Marston
(permission:
Bruce Fisher)

SARAH CATHERINE SHOLTER
MRS. JAMES SILVERWOOD MCPHERSON
b. March 23, 1833, Union Co, PA
d. June 9, 1888, Hartley Twsp, Union Co, PA
bur. Hironimus Union Church Cemetery, Weikert, Union Co, PA
dau. of John Sholter and Catherine Goodlander Sholter
mar. James Silverwood McPherson, March 9, 1859

Children: Emma (*mar. 1.* James Pursley, *mar. 2.* David Libby), William Isaac, Mary Catherine (*mar.* David C. Galer), Alda Lavina (*mar.* William Cromly), Charles Milton, Clarence Newton, Martha Harriet E. (*mar.* William McColm), Cora Bella (*mar.* David P. Galer), John Howard, Maggie May.
[F.A.G. 29579167]

Sarah C.
McPherson
(permission:
Bill Cunningham)

HANNAH M. SHOLTER
MRS. JOSEPH L. WALLACE
b. June 1844, Union Co, PA
d. around 1934, Hartley Township, Union Co, PA
bur. Grace Evangelical Church Cemetery, Laurelton, Union Co, PA

dau. of John Sholter and Catherine Goodlander Sholter

mar. Joseph L. Wallace, around 1881, Lewistown, Mifflin Co, PA

In 1850–80 in Hartley Township, around 1900 a short stay in Mifflin County.

Children: Charles E. (*bur.* Laurelton), Amanda R. (*b.* Weikert, *mar.* William H. Young), John Langton, Agnes Jean (*mar.* Clem Stimeling), Samuel.

MARY ELIZABETH SHOLTER
  MRS. GEORGE O. BARNET
b. Feb. 14, 1844, Hartley Twsp, Union Co, PA
d. Feb. 3, 1924
bur. Boltz Cemetery, Miller Co, Missouri
dau. of John Sholter and Catherine Goodlander Sholter
mar. George O. Barnet

In 1850 census she was living in the Benjamin Goodlander household. By 1866 they had moved to Miller County, Missouri. She is listed as Boltz rather than Sholter in the transcribing of the tombstone information.

Children (born in Missouri): Thomas J., Lucy J., Eva, Simon Henry, John M.

[F.A.G. 12499583]

MARY C. PURSLEY
  MRS. JOHN LEROY C. GOODLANDER
b. around 1850 or 1842, Hartley Twsp, Union Co, PA
d. around 1868, in Missouri or Kansas, following the birth of her son.
dau. of William P. Pursley and Eliza Switzer Pursley
mar. John L. C. Goodlander
  She was the first wife of John L. C. Goodlander.
  Children: Oscar Reed

ANNA AUMILLER
  MRS. WILLIAM F. JOHNSON
b. July, 1851 (tombstone says 1843)
d. Aug. 26, 1920, Glen Iron, Union Co, PA
bur. Hironimus Union Church Cemetery, Weikert, Union Co, PA
dau. of George J. Aumiller and Sarah Hartman (?) Aumiller
mar. William F. Johnson Jr., 1874

He was the railroad agent at Cherry Run. In 1900 census House 1, he was 56, she was 48. In 1914 William Johnson Jr. and Anna sold about 100 acres to the "Syndicate" of Moser, Witmer and McConnell.

Children (in 1900 census): Gainesville, 21, Charles, 14.

[F.A.G. 91836014]

Anna Johnson
(permission: Bill Cunningham)

CATHERINE SHIRK
MRS. JACOB F. BARNET
b. Jan. 10, 1836
d. Nov. 29, 1898
bur. Hironimus Union Church Cemetery, Weikert, Union Co, PA
mar. Jacob F. Barnet

Shirk also spelled Sherick. She had worked as a domestic servant for the John Barnet family and they farmed. Marriage certificate in Cora Boop's files.

Children: William F., John H.

[F.A.G. 91830331]

Catharine wife of Jacob Barnet
(permission: Bill Cunningham)

MARIA SARAH LOUISA GOODLANDER
    MRS. PHILIP C. FESSENDEN
b. Oct. 22, 1842, Weikert, Union Co, PA
d. Aug. 10, 1903, Hartley Twsp, Union Co, PA
bur. Lincoln Chapel Cemetery, Laurelton, Union Co, PA
dau. of John D. Goodlander and Margaret Goodlander
mar. Philip C. Fessenden
    Louisa in 1860 census.
    Children: James Lemuel (*b.* 1862, Weikert, PA).
    [F.A.G. 22584190]

Louisa M. Fessenden (permission: Philip F. Snyder)

JAMILLA GOODLANDER
    MRS. WILLIAM ECKLEY WEIKEL
b. 1848
d. 1895
bur. Lincoln Chapel Cemetery, Laurelton, Union Co, PA
dau. of Christian or Christopher Goodlander and Mary Osmond Goodlander
mar. William Eckley Weikel (*bur.* at New Berlin Cemetery, Union Co)

In 1868 a W. E. Weikel had property on the Weikert Road east of the center of town. Jamilia's parents both were buried at Milton Cemetery. In 1900 the Weikels—presumably a different wife—were listed as land owners in Hartley Township, and in 1901 they were members of Hironimus Union Church and contributors to the Church's Mission Fund.

    Children: Hannah (*b.* 1863, *d.* 1895, *mar.* D. C. Johnson).
    [F.A.G. 76842461]

MINA "MINNIE" HENRY
   MRS. PERCIVAL AUMILLER
b. May 1848/9, Centerville, Snyder Co, PA
d. 1930
bur. Long Lane Cemetery, Laurelton, Union Co, PA
mar. Percival "Percy" Aumiller

They had 450 acres along Penns Creek, now PA Fish Commission property "Aumiller Bottom."

Children: Aaron A., Wesley, Harriet "Hattie" (*mar.* Boop), Gertrude (*mar.* Dorman), Ada E. (*mar.* Katherman).

[F.A.G. 122080430]

Mena Aumiller (permission: Glenda Sheaffer)

JANE PARSONS
   MRS. DAVID GALER
b. Aug. 31, 1817, in Centre Co, PA
d. Sept. 11, 1893, Patch Grove, Wyalusing, Grant Co, Wisconsin
mar. David Galer, June 14, 1838, in Centre Co, PA

A Jane Galer was listed on White Springs Circuit Church roll.

Children: John (*b.* 1840 in PA), Sarah Jane (*b.* 1852 in PA), Elizabeth (*b.* 1853 in PA), Michael (*b.* 1858 in PA), Caroline (*b.* 1860 in PA).

SARAH ELIZABETH A. C. GOODLANDER
   MRS. ZACHARY T. GALER
b. April 7, 1851
d. Sept. 27, 1925
bur. Hironimus Union Church Cemetery, Weikert, Union Co, PA
dau. of Christian (Christopher in will) Goodlander and Jane C. Goodlander

mar. Zachary T. Galer, 1869

In 1874 they granted a lease to the railroad. In 1875 with the John Galers they sold 1 acre 110 perches to the railroad for $322.50.

Children (in 1900 census): John M., 21, George, 15.

[F.A.G. 88768030]

Sarah Goodlander Galer (permission: Bill Cunningham)

CATHERINE "KATE" GALER
MRS. GEORGE WASHINGTON AUMILLER
b. May 22, 1854, Hartley Twsp, Union Co, PA
d. Dec. 13, 1928, Hartley Twsp, Union Co, PA
bur. Troxelville Union Cemetery, Snyder Co, PA
dau. of John W. Galer Jr. and Jane Switzer Galer
mar. George Washington Aumiller, before 1880

She played the violin and accordion. A dignified friendly lady. Aumiller Genealogy says her father was born in Germany.

Children: John David, Flora (*mar.* Gill), Mary Jane, Catherine Elizabeth (*b.* 1884, *d.* 1942, *mar.* Folk), Carrie Mabel (*mar.* Lepley), Sarah Mae "Sadie" (*mar.* Sipe), Carbon Cleveland, William, Bertha Elsie (*mar.* Fetterolf).

[F.A.G. 114069612]

MARY LUCINDA HIRONIMUS
MRS. JAMES L. LIBBY
b. July 22, 1862
d. Jan. 11, 1887
bur. Hironimus Union Church Cemetery, Weikert, Union Co, PA
dau. of Andrew Hironimus and Lucinda Burns Hironimus

mar. James L. Libby, his first wife
   [F.A.G. 88756145]

Mary L. wife of
James Libby
(permission:
Bill Cunningham)

Minnie Dorman
   Mrs. Edward Embeck
b. April 14, 1862 (tombstone says 1888)
d. Dec. 22, 1941
bur. Old Cedars Cemetery, Swengel, Union Co, PA
dau. of Henry Franklin Dorman and Hannah Mary Bridge Dorman (Henry's second wife) or Lizzie Zimmerman (first wife)
mar. Edward Embeck, July 8, 1906

Her parents had property along Penns Creek in Weikert. In 1907/8 she taught Sunday school and was a member of the Sunday School Bible Class at Hironimus Union Church. In 1910 living in Millmont, Union Co, PA. In 1920 living in Lewis Twsp, Union Co, PA.
   [F.A.G. 89006340]

Mary Jane "Jennie" Aumiller
   Mrs. John E. Rheppard
b. March 31, 1869
d. Jan. 14, 1894
bur. Hironimus Union Church Cemetery, Weikert, Union Co, PA
dau. of George Michael Aumiller and Sarah Hartman Aumiller
mar. John E. Rheppard

Children: Charles G. Rheppard (*b.* 1886), Estella (Reppert, *b.* 1891, *mar.* Dauberman), and two more.
   [F.A.G. 88754356]

Mary wife of
John Rheppard
(permission:
Bill Cunningham)

SARAH FIETTA "SALLIE" SWANK
  MRS. JAMES K. PURSLEY
b. April 2, 1852, Lewis Twsp, Snyder Co, PA
d. March 15, 1933, Philadelphia, PA
bur. Hartleton Cemetery, Hartley Twsp, Union Co, PA
mar. James K. Pursley, 1866

She married at age 15. In 1875 they sold 1 acre and 89 perches to the railroad for $62.50. Sarah and James moved from Weikert to Laurelton with their eight children in the early 1890s. She was a member of White Springs UMC Circuit.

Children: William (*b.* Aug. 11, 1869, *mar.* Carrie, *b.* 1876, *d.* 1925), Aminda "Minnie" (*b.* Aug. 15, 1872, *mar.* Glover), David Reed "Pete" (*b.* Jan. 3, 1874), Harry R. "Bob" (*mar.* Ann Hare, *b.* 1888, *d.* 1946), Mary Ellen (*b.* June 4, 1867, *mar.* Crouse), Eliza "Lida" (*b.* March 6, 1876, *mar.* Helwig), Sarah "Sady" (*b.* July 7, 1879), James Geddes (*b.* Dec. 1, 1881, *bap.* Dec. 17, 1882, White Springs UMC Circuit), Helen. Minnie, David, Eliza, Mary, Sady and William *bap.* Nov. 8, 1879, White Springs UMC Circuit.

[F.A.G. 16511091]

NANCY JANE ZIMMERMAN
  MRS. ALLEN SEYMOUR JOLLY
b. Feb. 10, 1847, Union Co, PA
d. March 17, 1931, Pardee, Union Co, PA
bur. Hironimus Union Church Cemetery, Weikert, Union Co, PA
dau. of Jesse Zimmerman and Mary Holler Zimmerman
mar. Allen Seymour Jolly, April 29, 1866

In 1900 census House 21, she was a 53-year-old widow living with her son Edward; they were tenants. She smoked a pipe (as witnessed by Clark Shively).

Children: Frank S. (*b.* 1868), Margaret N. (*b.* 1869, *mar.* Weller?), Minerva "Minnie" May (*b.* 1872, *mar. 1.* Whatmore, *mar. 2.* Kaler), Edward. F. (*b.* 1874), Sarah "Sadie" J. (*b.* 1875, *mar.* Stump), Hattie B. (*b.* 1879, *mar. 1.* Sholter, *mar. 2.* Tharp), Melvin C. (*b.* 1884).

Nancy J. Jolley
(permission:
Bill Cunningham)

ANNIE A. BENNEY
    MRS. HENRY BUFFINGTON
    MRS. FRANK BOOP
b. Dec. 8, 1869, Baltimore, Maryland
d. July 1, 1918, Union Co, PA
bur. Lincoln Chapel Cemetery, Laurelton, Union Co, PA
dau. of David Benney and Araminda Johnson Benny
mar. 1. Henry Buffington
mar. 2. Frank Boop, May 25, 1899, his second wife

In 1900 census House 94. Frank was 45, she was 29. He was *bur.* Hironimus Union Church Cemetery, Weikert, Union Co, PA.

Children: Edward Lewis, Harry A. ("Babe," *b.* 1895, *d.* Feb. 26, 1896, age 5 months 15 days), David James, William Reno, Laura Alice Boop (*b.* 1900, *d.* 1948, *mar.* Feaster).

[F.A.G. 76546904]

Annie A. wife
of Frank Boop
(permission:
Waterfall)

SARAH ALICE KATHERMAN
   MRS. ALANSON JOHNSON
b. July 14, 1855, Hartley Twsp, Union Co, PA
d. April 18, 1931, Hartley Twsp, Union Co, PA
bur. Hartleton Cemetery, Union Co, PA
dau. of John F. Katherman and Susan Williams Katherman
mar. Alanson Johnson, April 11, 1872

They lived at "Avian Haven," 8035 Weikert Road, Weikert. She was an aunt of John Krumrine, who with his wife, Tome Hosterman Krumrine, lived on the farm that became the CCC Camp and later the Union County Sportsmen's Club.

Children: Albert Williams (*b.* Nov. 28, 1872, Weikert, *mar. 1.* Dora Miller, Nov. 1893, New Berlin, Union Co, PA, *mar. 2.* Mary C. Steck, 1913), Elmer Elsworth (*b.* Sept. 28, 1875), Susie (*mar.* Showalter), Minnie Elizabeth May (*mar.* Boop), Miles Warren, Nellie Viola (*mar.* Bowersox). Albert and Elmer *bap.* 1979, White Springs UMC Circuit.

   [F.A.G. 10410917]

ROSE (ROSA) LOUISA GOODLANDER
   MRS. ALBERT NEWTON BITNER
b. April 21, 1874, Weikert, Union Co, PA
d. Jan. 16,. 1951, Milton, Northumberland Co, PA
bur. Lincoln Chapel Cemetery, Laurelton, Union Co, PA
dau. of John L. Goodlander and Jennie Virginia Quinlan Goodlander
mar. Albert Newton Bitner, Sept. 24, 1896

   [F.A.G. 38694855]

SARAH "SADIE" JANE JOLLY
   MRS. JOHN STUMP
   MRS. AMBROSE BETTILYON
   MRS. JOHN BOOP
b. June 6, 1875, Oil City, Venango Co, PA
d. Dec. 22, 1967, Hartleton, Union Co, PA
bur. Hartleton Cemetery, Union Co, PA
dau. of Allen Seymour Jolly and Nancy J. Zimmerman Jolly
mar. 1. John Stump
mar. 2. Ambrose Bettilyon (Almose Bethlehem), Aug. 4, 1932
mar. 3. John Boop

In 1900 census age 24, living with brother Ed Jolly and wife Mary. Member of Hironimus Union Church. In 1940 census House 1: Ambrose was 66, she was 64. In 1967, Hironimus Church Memory List.
   [F.A.G. 104110028]

Sadie Boop looking at burned trailer in Millmont (permission: Tony Shively)

LUCINDA "LUCY" BURNS
   MRS. ANDREW HIRONIMUS
b. April 25, 1840
d. Aug. 12, 1920
bur. Hironimus Union Church Cemetery, Weikert, Union Co, PA
dau. of George Burns and Lucinda Auchmuty Burns
mar. Andrew Hironimus, July 25, 1861, Laurelton, Union Co, PA

In 1875 they sold 61 perches to the railroad for $21.25. In 1876 they leased land to the railroad and also granted land to the railroad. In 1880 census House 21, given as Louisa Anna, age 40. In 1880 they gave land along with the Barnetts for the Hironimus Union Church. In 1900 census House 12, he was 62, she was 60, nephew Andrew H., 19. In 1904 they deeded burial lots to Jacob Barnett. In 1908 she was a member of the Sunday School Bible Class at the Hironimus Union Church.

Children: Mary Lucinda (*mar.* James Libby, his first wife), Sarah Alice (*mar.* Charles Brown, 1904, in Oklahoma), John William (*mar.* Ellen Freed), Anna Elizabeth (*mar.* James Libby, his second wife), George Burns (*mar.* Anna M. Kleckner), Hannah Jane (*mar.* Alvin Boop), Eva Regina (*mar.* Frank Jolly), Ellen B. or Maggie (*mar.* Emmett Weiand, moved to Elysburg by 1910), Samuel Jacob (*d.* at 3 months), Kathryn "Kate" (*mar.* John Sholter), Ida Bell (*d.* under one year), Andrew James (*mar.* Bertha Rote), Franklin Perry (*d.* at three years), Charlotte May (*mar. 1.* John Irwin, *mar. 2.* George Zeckman).

[F.A.G. 88765005]

(permission: Boop/Wirt)

ELIZABETH SCHNURE
   MRS. FOSTER W. MCCURDY
b. 1841?
d. Aug. 28, 1895
bur. Keister Cemetery, Weikert, Union Co, PA
dau. of Christian Schnure and Lydia Keister Schnure
mar. Foster W. McCurdy

In 1875 Foster and wife Elizabeth sold 1 acre 50 perches to the railroad for $83.75.

Children: Jennie (? *mar.* Wesley Fairchild)
[F.A.G. 122015722]

Elizabeth wife of
Foster W. McCurdy
(permission:
Bruce Fisher)

AGNES JANE AIKEY
   MRS. BENJAMIN F. SHOLTER
b. Jan. 30, 1855, Hartleton, Union Co, PA
d. Feb. 1, 1921, Bellefonte, Centre Co, PA
bur. Hartleton Cemetery, Hartleton, Union Co, PA
dau. of Thomas J. Aikey and Elvina (or Lavina) Catherman Aikey
mar. Benjamin F. Sholter, Jan. 24, 1876

He was a railroad section hand, and she was a boarding house operator. They lived on White Mountain Road, Weikert, PA. In 1900 census House 23, he was 44, she was 46, Sadie, 18, Daniel, 16, Ralph, 14, plus Elvina Kline, 23, and grandson (William F. Kline). In 1903 she was a Sunday school class member and teacher at Hironimus Union Church. In the early 1900s she gave a donation to Hironimus Union Church for mission work. 1921 Letter of Administration, Union County Court House.

Children: Sadie (*mar.* Alfred File?), William David (*b.* Jan 5, 1874), Elvina (*b.* Oct. 8, 1876, *mar.* Kline), Agnes Jane (*b.* Dec. 8, 1881, *bap.* Feb. 24, 1884, White Springs UMC Circuit), Ella/Ellen V. (*b.* 1876, *mar.* Morris Long), Carey Daniel (*b.* 1883), Ralph Clarence (*b.* 1886). William and Elvina *bap.* Nov. 29, 1879, White Springs UMC Circuit.

[F.A.G. 10411353]

ALICE CATHERINE SHIELDS
   MRS. CHARLES W. GALER?
b. Nov. 17, 1876
d. 1961
bur. Hummelstown Cemetery, Hummelstown, Dauphin Co, PA

dau. of Felix Shields and Annie M. Shields
mar. Galer

Lived at Cherry Run, Weikert Road, Weikert. On Nov. 12, 1879, *bap.* White Springs UMC Circuit.

[F.A.G. 13712584]

Sarah Alice Benny
    Mrs. Oliver Catherman
b. Nov. 28, 1876, Maryland
d. Sept. 4, 1959, Union Co, PA
bur. Hartleton Cemetery, Hartleton, Union Co, PA
dau. of David Benney and Araminda Johnson Benney
mar. Oliver Catherman

She was raised by John and Susan Catherman after Araminda abandoned the children. John was an uncle to her husband Oliver.

Children: Grace Mathilda "Tillie" (*mar.* Folk), Harold Thomas.

[F.A.G. 10410103]

Nancy A. Galer?
    Mrs. George W. Kreisher
b. around 1845
mar. George W. Kreisher (Krisher)

He was listed as a railroad repair laborer. In 1877 they owned land along the Weikert Road. In 1880 they lived between Mary Bettleyon and George Aumiller. In 1897 she owned 6 acres 125 perches near William Johnson at Penns Creek.

Children: Clarence Adam (*b.* Oct. 11, 1874, *bap.* July 6, 1879, White Springs UMC Circuit), Eva Elletta (*b.* Feb. 5, 1878, *bap.* July 6, 1879), Cora May (*b.* July 24, 1880, *bap.* Dec. 21, 1881), Regina Clare (*b.* Aug. 10, 1884, *bap.* April 23, 1885).

Bertha Louise Goodlander
    Mrs. James Daniel Bilger
b. May 9, 1888, Weikert, Hartley Twsp, Union Co, PA
d. Nov. 22, 1976, Union Co, PA
bur. Hironimus Union Church Cemetery, Weikert, Union Co, PA
dau. of Oscar Reed Goodlander and Harriet "Clara" Clark Goodlander
mar. James Daniel Bilger Sr., April 9, 1904, Laurelton, Union Co, PA

Bertha at three months old was the first child baptized at Hironimus Union Church. She was on the church memory list for 1976. Her mother "Clara" Goodlander raised ten children on the farm near the church. In 1920 census Bertha and James Bilger lived in House 2.

Children: Robert E. or B., James Daniel Jr., Maude E., Helen C., Martha V., Leona, Rose, Doris and May. Harriet died in infancy; Bertha, *d.* 1908, age 3.

[F.A.G. 91832400]

Bertha L. Bilger
(permission:
Bill Cunningham)

ALICE (BRIDGE)

She is mentioned on the White Springs UMC membership roll along with George, Jeremiah (expelled 1878) and Mary Bridge.

ARMINDA JOHNSON
   MRS. DAVID BENNY (OR BENNEY)
bur. Woodmere Memorial Park, Huntingdon, Cabell Co, West Virginia
dau. of William Johnson Sr. and Catherine Switzer Johnson
mar. 1. David Benny, Oct. 29, 1867, Baltimore, Maryland, *div.* April 24, 1909.
mar. 2. (?) Theodore Freed
mar. 3. J. M. Blankenship

On May 15, 1879, Arminda (Araminda, Armanda) was Postmaster at Cherry Run, listed as "Penny." She was mentioned in White Springs Church circuit membership roll. She was said to be an excellent midwife. She left in 1886 with Freed to Baltimore taking only daughter Ida. She later married Blankenship but never lived with him, lived with her daughter Ida Reid. Arminda's divorce papers in Union County Courthouse, Lewisburg, PA, cover years 1890 to 1909).

Children: Anna Benny (*b.* 1868, *d.* 1918, *mar.* Boop), MaryBelle "Molly" "Mame" (*b.* 1870, *mar.* Rearick), Catherine V. Benney (*b.* 1871, *d.* 1877, *bur.*

Keister Cemetery, Hartley Twsp, Union Co, PA), Minnie Benney (*b.* 1873, *d.* 1928, *mar.* Fuhrman), Sarah Alice Benney (*b.* 1876, *mar.* Catherman), Joseph Cees Binney/Benny (*b.* May 17, 1879, *bap.* White Springs UMC circuit, *d.* 1893), Laura Benney (*b.* 1882, *d.* 1980, *mar.* Wikel), Ida Benney (*b.* 1886, *d.* 1964, Huntingdon, West Virginia, *mar.* Reid).
[F.A.G. 63614122 or 58463763]

CARRIE C. SHOLTER
   MRS. HERBERT KEENE
   MRS. OSCAR A. PURSLEY
b. Aug. 22, 1877 or 1879, Weikert, Union Co, PA
d. Dec. 25, 1963, Carbon Co, PA
bur. Franklin Heights Memorial Park, East Weissport, Carbon Co, PA
dau. of George Washington Sholter and Elizabeth M. Buffington Sholter
mar. 1. Herbert Keene, Aug. 3, 1899, *div.* May 25, 1912
mar. 2. Oscar A. Pursley
   In 1899 she taught Sunday school at Hironimus Union Church.
   Children: Elizabeth Keene
   [F.A.G. 90521356]

SARAH ANN MARTIN
   MRS. HENRY A. SHOLTER
b. Sept, around 1843 or 1833
d. around 1901
mar. Henry A. Sholter
   Lived in Weikert from around 1880. Much of the family was at times in Pocohontas, West Virginia. In 1900 census House 40: she was a widow, age 56.
   Children (in 1900 census): Samuel, 21, Perry Clayton, 19, Amanda, 17, Alice, 14, Thomas W.

ANNIE M. (SHIELDS)
   MRS. FELIX SHIELDS
b. 1859, in PA
mar. Felix Shields
   Lived at Cherry Run, Weikert Road, Weikert, next to George Sheesley between William Johnson and Mary Bettleyon. Felix was born in Ireland in 1845. He was listed on census as a farm laborer. In 1880 census she was 21.

Women of Weikert

In 1897 she owned 31 perches, and in 1900 she was on the Hartley Township landowner's list. She was a member of White Springs UMC Circuit.

Children: William Henry (*b.* April 10, 1875), Alice Catherine (*b.* Nov. 17, 1876, *mar.* Galer), John Elmer (*b.* March 31, 1879). They were *bap.* Nov. 12, 1879, White Springs UMC Circuit.

EMMA JANE C. MCPHERSON
  MRS. WILLIAM A. PURSLEY
  MRS. DAVID LIBBY
b. Aug. 1 or 5, 1863 or 1865, Winfield, Union Co, PA
d. 1950
bur. Hironimus Union Church Cemetery, Weikert, Union Co, PA
dau. of James Silverwood McPherson and Sarah Catherine Sholter McPherson
mar. 1. William A. Pursley, 1880, his second wife
mar. 2. David Libby, 1892

Lived at 5570 Weikert Road, Weikert, PA. In 1900 census House 55, he was 31, she was 36. In 1928 she was a Sunday school teacher at Hironimus Union Church.

Children (in 1900 census): Bertha Ann Pursley, 17, James William Pursley, 16.

[F.A.G. 91836518]

(permission: Tim Bastian)

HANNAH MARY WEIKEL
   MRS. DAVID CRAWFORD JOHNSON
b. Feb. 25, 1863
d. April 18, 1895
bur. Hironimus Union Church Cemetery, Weikert, Union Co, PA
dau. of William Weikel (of Glen Iron, PA)
mar. David Crawford Johnson, 1880, his first wife.

They had a store at Lindale on what is now Sholter land. She died 30 days after Arthur was born.

Children: Maud (*b.* 1882), Ray Lee (*b.* 1884), Grace M. (*b.* 1888), Harold B. (*b.* 1892), Arthur F. (*b.* 1895).
   [F.A.G. 76842461]

Hannah M. wife of
D. C. Johnson
(permission:
Bill Cunningham)

ELIZABETH "LIZZIE" HOSTETLER
   MRS. PERRY L. GRUBB
b. March 9, around 1854/64, McAlisterville, Juniata Co, PA
d. Oct. 1, 1937, Altoona, Blair Co, PA
bur. Rosehill Cemetery, Altoona, Blair Co, PA
dau. of David Hostetler and Sarah Smith Hostetler
mar. Perry L. Grubb, Aug. 1877

In 1880 they lived between John Longer and Theodore Freed (in Lindale?). He signed the Articles of the Hironimus Union Church. They moved to Altoona in 1889 and lived at 119 4th St. He worked for the Pennsylvania Railroad for 33 years. They were married at least 57 years (*Altoona Tribune*, Aug. 13, 1934).

Children: Charles E. Grubb (*b.* 1883, *d.* 1938)
   [F.A.G. 144926126]

Mary H. Bettilyon
Mrs. Alvah W. Longer
b. around 1854
mar. Alvah W. Longer, his second wife

Lived at 7715 Weikert Rd., Weikert. In 1880 census lived near George Sheesley and William Johnson; children were Ambrose, 10, Lillie J., 6. In 1920 census House 3, he was 61, she was 68, with Ambrose D., 47, widowed, William O., 21, Amber M., 14, George E., 12, James L., 9; also David Benny, 68, widowed. In 1930 census W. Alvah Leonger, 73, with wife Annie K. Leonger.

Children: Ambrose D., Lillie J., William O., Amber M., George E., James L.

Nancy (Wallace)
Mrs. Job Wallace
b. around 1824
mar. Job Wallace

In 1880, as widow age 56, she lived near Zach Galer and Charles Marston.

Children: Margaret (*d.* at age 19, *bur.* Keister Cemetery?)

Margaret (Bridge)
Mrs. George Bridge
mar. George Bridge

In 1880 census lived between Thomas Libby and Alvah Marston. George is buried in Lewisburg Cemetery.

Children): Jacob, 13, Margaret, 11, Merrit, 9, Lewis, 7, Edward, 5.

Mary Ann (Bridge)
Mrs. William H. Bridge
b. around 1850/9, Union Co, PA
d. 1920
bur. Lewisburg Cemetery, Lewisburg, Union Co, PA
mar. William H. Bridge

In 1880 in Weikert they lived between Thomas Libby and Alvah Marston. At one time they were living next door to George and Margaret Bridge. She is on a White Springs Church roll.

[F.A.G. 105351685]

BERTHA "BERTIE" ANN PURSLEY
　MRS. CYRUS H. LAHR
b. Aug. 25, 1882
d. 1956, in California
bur. Hironimus Union Church Cemetery, Weikert, Union Co, PA
dau. of William Pursley and Emma McPherson (stepdaughter of David Libby)
mar. Cyrus H. Lahr, *div.* Aug. 28, 1914

In 1882 baptized at White Springs Church. She was a member of the Hironimus Union Church. In 1956 her body was brought home from California by train. She was remembered on the Hironimus Union Church Memory List.
　[F.A.G. 99956127]

Bertha Pursley Lahr (permission: Bill Cunningham)

MARY ALICE SHOLTER
　MRS. WILLIAM STIMELING
b. 1860
d. 1942
bur. Hartleton Cemetery, Hartleton, Union Co, PA
dau. of Henry Sholter Sr.?
mar. William Stimeling

He is listed as Stimbling on Laurelton Center reports. They were living at Cherry Run, Weikert, in 1882. In 1900 census House 84. Alice Stimeling, landowner, 60 (*sic*), also David Bowersox, 77, in household. Also in 1900 census, William Stimeling, 38, is in Samuel Frederick's household; Sam is 61, his daughter Alice, 35, and her husband Charles Boop, 22. In 1930 census House 153, Alice, a widow, is 65 (*sic*).

　Children: Clemuel "Clem" (*b.* July 18, 1886, *bap.* Aug. 30, 1896, White Springs UMC Circuit, *mar.* Agnes Jean Wallace), Wesley Reno (*b.* Jan. 6,

1891), Florence "Flora" Bertha (*b.* Feb. 23, 1895, *mar.* Charles Sampsell), John Bolich. Wesley and Florence *bap.* Sept. 22, 1897, White Springs UMC Circuit.

[F.A.G. 10411395]

MINERVA "MINNIE" JORDAN
    MRS. REED T. PURSLEY
b. March 1852, Wharton, Potter Co, PA
d. Jan. 1937
bur. Hironimus Union Church Cemetery, Weikert, Union Co, PA
mar. Reed T. Pursley, around 1882

On Feb. 22, 1888, Reed and Minnie sold 3 acres along the creek to Henry Dorman. In 1900 census House 20; he was 45, she was 36. In 1910 census House 16; he was 55, she was 45. In 1913–14, 1917 and 1920, she taught Sunday school at Hironimus Union Church. In 1915–23 she was Postmaster at Weikert in her home (obituary says for 29 years).

Children (in 1910 census): Oscar C., 26, John A., 23, Samuel A., 22, Mary L. (*mar.* C. D. Cook), 17, Warren B., 13, William, 10, James L., 8, Charles W., 6, Clara A. (*mar.* Boop), 1.

[F.A.G. 91848128]

Minnie Pursley
(permission: Bill Cunningham)

ELIZABETH GALER
    MRS. ALVAH MARSTON
b. around 1853
dau. of David Galer and Jane Parsons Galer
mar. Alvah Marston Jr., Union Co, PA

Lived in Weikert and then moved to Kansas in 1883. In 1880 census her birth year is given as 1843.

Children: Eugene (*d.* Sept. 12, 1872, *bur.* Keister Cemetery).

SARAH "SADIE" LIBBY
   MRS. WILLIAM BAYLOR
   MRS. LAWRENCE BROUSE
b. around 1884
dau. of James Libby and Annie Hironimus Libby
mar. 1. William Baylor
mar. 2. Lawrence Brouse

   In 1899 she was the Hironimus Sunday School librarian..
   Children: Arabel Baylor, William Baylor; Harold Brouse, William Brouse, Helen Brouse.

CHESTIA ALVERTA SHOLTER
   MRS. HARRY ARTHUR WALLS
b. Dec. 27, 1868
d. June 19, 1953
bur. Long Lane Cemetery, Laurelton, Union Co, PA
dau. of Henry A. Sholter and Sarah Ann Martin Sholter
mar. Harry Arthur Walls, March 5, 1885

   Lived at Cherry Run in 1889.
   Children: John Arthur Walls (*mar. 2.* Minnie E. Johnson), Sarah Catherine (*mar.* Melvin C. Jolly); they were twins, born in 1889.
   [F.A.G. 122080821]

Chestia A. wife of
Harry A. Walls
(permission:
Jane Ely Foster)

AMANDA CHRISTINE DERR
   MRS. JACOB FRANKLIN SPACHT
b. April 14, 1843/4, Luzerne Co, PA
d. Aug. 21, 1934, Union Co, PA

bur. Hironimus Union Church Cemetery, Weikert, Union Co, PA
mar. Jacob Franklin Spach(t), 1866

She was from near Middleburg. He was the last surviving Civil War Veteran of the "West End." Around 1885 they moved to Pardee, where they had a store. In 1900 census House 49, he was 54, she was 56. They raised their granddaughter Margaret "Maggie" Galer Hironimus (*mar.* James).

Children: 1 daughter and 3 sons.

[F.A.G. 91848321]

(permission: Tony Shively)

IDA SEYMOUR FREED
   MRS. DANIEL CARY LIBBY
   MRS. JAMES LIBBY
b. Nov. 4, 1868, Mifflin Co, PA
d. April 14, 1938, Hartley Twsp, Union Co, PA
bur. Hironimus Union Church Cemetery, Weikert, Union Co, PA
dau. of Theodore Gund (Freed) and Selena Isabelle Corbin Gund (Freed)
mar. 1. Daniel Cary Libby Sr., 1885
mar. 2. James Libby, separated (over a family affair)

She operated a boarding house. In 1900 census House 7. Daniel was 35, she was 31. In 1910 census House 11. She was 41, widowed, and head of household. Her PA death certificate (no. 39139) gives her maiden name as Gund.

Children (in 1900 census): Theodore (Thomas?), 13, George Ralph, 10, William Sherwood, 8, Daniel, 6, Lyman, 4, Dewey, 1, Margaret or Marguerite (*mar.* Keister), Cora (*mar.* Price), Wealthy (*mar.* Morrow), Virginia (*mar.* Bettilyon).

[F.A.G. 91827646]

(permission: Wirt/Boop)

MARY ANN SAXTON
 MRS. ABRAHAM FREED
b. May 15, 1815, Silver Spring Twsp, Cumberland Co, PA
d. March 13, 1885, Lewisburg, Union Co, PA, of pneumonia
bur. Hironimus Union Church Cemetery, Weikert, Union Co, PA
mar. Abraham Freed
 Children: Theodore Freed, William M. Freed. She was the grandmother of Mary Ellen Freed Hironimus, who *mar.* John William Hironimus.
 [F.A.G. 29836273

ELIZABETH JENKINS
 MRS. JOHN M. GALER
 MRS. JOHN BARNETT
b. Nov. 17, 1886, Johnstown
d. July 18, 1972, Johnstown
bur. Evangelical United Brethren (now Faith UMC) Cemetery, Belsano, PA
dau. of Ambrose Jenkins and Emma Shomo Jenkins
mar. 1. John M. Galer (*d.* 1933)
mar. 2. John Barnett, in late 1930s (*d.* late 1940s)
 She was a survivor of the Johnstown Flood of 1889. Her first husband was a native of the Weikert area, a son of David C. Galer. She continued to live in the Weikert area and also part-time with daughters in Johnstown area.
 Children: Howard, Ethel (*mar.* Palensar), Florence "Fay," Nora, Sara "Sallie" (*mar.* Sholter).

(permission: Jerry Sholter)

CORA LOUISE SHOLTER
    MRS. SIMON SHOWALTER BINGAMAN
b. Nov. 17, 1887, Weikert, Union Co, PA
d. June 30, 1970, Lewisburg, Union Co, PA
bur. Hironimus Union Church Cemetery, Weikert, Union Co, PA
dau. of William Sholter and Mary Salone Specht Sholter
mar. Simon Showalter Bingaman, June 13, 1907, Laurelton, Union Co, PA

"Sime" and "Mrs. Sime" lived at 5525 Weikert Road, Weikert, PA. In 1970 she was on the Hironimus Union Church memory list.

Children: William Orvis (*b.* Jan 18, 1908), Glydia "Gladys" Geraldine (*b.* Dec. 8, 1911, *mar.* Harvey), Simon Frederick (*b.* Nov. 26, 1913), Isabel Virginia (*b.* Oct. 20, 1915, *mar.* Badinger), Earl M. (*b.* Aug. 30, 1917), Rhoda Mae (*b.* Oct. 30, 1920, *mar.* Nale), Daniel J., Everitt V., Ruth Aletta, Mary Lou. Dates of birth from record of baptism on June 22, 1922, in White Springs UMC Circuit.

[F.A.G. 122080453]

(permission: Danny Harvey)

GRACE M. JOHNSON
b. April 14, 1888
d. Oct. 12, 1967
bur. Long Lane Cemetery, Laurelton, Union Co, PA
dau. of David Crawford Johnson and Hannah Mary Weikel

In 1900 census she was 12. In 1906/8 she was a member of the Hironimus Union Church Sunday School Bible Class. Grace was a member of Eastern Star. A graduate of Laurelton High School, New Berlin Seminary and Bloomsburg State Normal School, she taught in Union County for five years and became a teacher at the Bellefonte High School, Bellefonte, Centre County, PA. In 1967 she was listed on the Hironimus Union Church Memory Roll.

[F.A.G. 122080588]

Grace M. Johnson
(permission: Jane Ely Foster)

ANN ELIZABETH HIRONIMUS
  MRS. JAMES LIBBY
b. Jan. 10, 1868
d. Nov. 19, 1912
bur. Long Lane Cemetery, Laurelton, Union Co, PA
dau. of Andrew Hironimus and Lucinda Burns Hironimus
mar. James Libby, 1888, his second wife

In 1900 census House 9, he was 37, she was 32, with children from his first marriage: Sadie J. (*mar. 1.* Baylor/Bailer, *mar. 2.* Brouse), 16, Hattie (*mar.* Keister), 14, Phineas H., 12, Francis C., 10, Harvey J., 9, Mary E. (*mar.* Swanger), 5, David M., 3, John Russell.

Children: David McKinly (*b.* Jan. 29, 1897, *bap.* June 12, 1897, White Springs UMC Circuit).

[F.A.G. 122080647]

Women of Weikert

MINERVA MAE "MINNIE" JOLLY
  MRS. WILLIAM HENRY WHATMORE
  MRS. WILLIAM KALER
b. July 28, 1872, Oil City, Venango Co, PA
d. March 22, 1957, Millmont, Lewis Twsp, Union Co, PA
bur. Hedrick Union Cemetery, East Conemaugh, Cambria Co, PA
dau. of Allen Jolly and Nancy Zimmerman Jolly
mar. 1. William Henry Whatmore, Dec. 24, 1887, Union Co, PA
mar. 2. William Kaler, Oct. 3, 1934, Lewisburg, Union Co, PA

Living at Cherry Run in 1888. In 1900 census William was 37, Minnie was 27.

Children (in 1900 census): Franklin H., 11, Estella Mae, 8, Daisy Irene, 5, Benjamin Allen, 2, Mary Helen, 3 months, 1 deceased child, then Anna Elizabeth, John Melvin, Charles Sylvester, Viola.

[F.A.G. 86618618]

SELINA ISABELLE CORBIN
  MRS. THEODORE FREED
b. 1847, Mifflin Co, PA?
d. 1898
bur. Hironimus Union Church Cemetery, Weikert, Union Co, PA
mar. Theodore Freed (separated)

Lived at Lindale. By 1890 Theodore was living with Araminda Johnson Benny. David Benny named Isabelle in the divorce proceedings (Union County Court records).

Children: Ida Seymour (*mar. 1.* Daniel Carey Libby Sr., *mar.* 2. James Libby), Mary Ellen Freed (*mar.* Hironimus).

[F.A.G. 91834073]

S. Isabelle Freed
nee Corbin
(permission:
Bill Cunningham)

BESSIE MARGARET "BESS" HIRONIMUS
    MRS. AMMON JOHN SHAFFER
b. Dec. 9, 1890, Weikert, Union Co, PA
d. June 9, 1967, Millmont, Union Co, PA
bur. Hironimus Union Church Cemetery, Weikert, Union Co, PA
dau. of John William Hironimus and Mary Ellen Freed Hironimus
mar. Ammon John Shaffer, after 1920

Lived on Weikert Road in Lindale. In 1910 she worked as a servant for the Hartman family. In 1920 she worked as housekeeper for the elder Shaffers. Bess was also "involved in business." She was known for baking wonderful pies, cakes, and large sugar cookies. Lewisburg-Tyrone trains would frequently stop so that passengers and railroaders could buy her baked goods. She always made peach pies for Bob Jolly. Jerry Sholter remembers his father George giving Bess cigarettes when they passed her place while deer spotting: Bess had her two fingers up at her mouth so that they could see her need (this being the universal sign for "out of smokes").

[F.A.G. 91828230]

(permission: Geri Willen)

ELLA or ELLEN (JOHNSON)
    MRS. WILLIAM JOHNSON
mar. William Johnson

In 1890 on Jan. 2 she sued William Johnson Sr. in Union County Court. In 1892 she sold lands to A. S. Jolly.

MINNIE ELVA JOHNSON
    MRS. JOHN ARTHUR WALLS
b. 1891 or 1889
d. Feb. 28, 1961, Hartley Twsp, Union Co, PA

bur. Hartleton Hill Cemetery, Hartleton, Union Co, PA
dau. of William Johnson
mar. 1. William Kaler (son of John Kaler and Sarah Bridge)?
mar. 2. John Arthur Walls, his second wife

Minnie had at least four children before marrying John Walls, including Elda M., her executrix. In 1921 her father gave Minnie 3+ acres near Cherry Run. She purchased land from her brother Lewis Johnson for $1, part of the land belonging to her father William Johnson when he died. John Arthur Walls, son of Harry A. and Chestia Alverta Sholter Walls, died at the home of his twin sister Sarah C. Jolly at Millmont. On Aug. 6, 1951, Minnie and her husband sold to Edwin F. Smith and Annie E. Smith of Shamokin a two-story frame cottage in the Cherry Run area bounded by the railroad on one side. According to 1961 Will Book, Union County Courthouse, Minnie E. Johnson Walls of Johnstown, Cambria Co, PA, left 26 acres with farm and building to her children Elda and Paul, $500 to her son George, $1 to her stepson Dayton Walls.

Children: Elda M. (*mar.* Marcinko), Paul, George.

HANNAH MARY BRIDGE
MRS. HENRY FRANKLIN DORMAN
b. Sept. 2, 1862, Lewisburg, Union Co, PA
d. Jan. 9, 1945, Lewis Twsp, Union Co, PA
bur. Old Cedars Cemetery, Swengel, Union Co, PA
dau. of George Bridge and Margaret Stevenson Bridge
mar. Henry Franklin Dorman, widower of Lizzie Zimmerman, after 1891(?)

They owned land along Penns Creek, now Jolly's Grove Lane, then moved to the family homestead just west of the Millmont bridge. They lived on land next to Jacob and Jonas Barnet. In 1899 a son David, 14, was killed by a train. In 1900 census House 18, he was 42, she was 37, Lewis (Louis E.), 18, Minnie, 12, Samuel, 8, George, 2. In 1909 Hannah and Henry sold small piece of ground along the creek. In 1910 they were living in Lewis Twsp, Union Co. In 1909 "Sister" Mary Dorman taught a Sunday School Class at Hironimus Union Church.

Children: Lincoln(?), Lewis Ellsworth, George, David, Minnie (*mar.* Embeck), William, Samuel Peter, Luther, Daniel Lawrence, Miriam A. (Marion) (*mar.* Bailey), Grace Margaret (*mar.* Catherman).

[F.A.G. 75102062]

ELIZA (JOHNSON)
    MRS. WILLIAM JOHNSON
mar. William Johnson
    Children: Minnie Elizabeth Johnson (*b.* Oct. 18, 1876, *bap.* June 23, 1892, White Springs Church).

JENNIE VIRGINIA QUINLAN
    MRS. JOHN LEROY C. GOODLANDER
    MRS. THOMAS H. EISENHUTH
b. July 25/26, 1854 or 1855, PA
d. July 13/14, 1934 or 1938
bur. Lincoln Chapel Cemetery, Laurelton, Union Co, PA
dau. of (Dr.) Quinlan and Katherine Thompson Quinlan
mar. 1. John Leroy C. Goodlander, before 1874
mar. 2. Thomas H. Eisenhuth, 1896

Thomas was listed as a railroad laborer and section foreman. They lived by Shreck's along the railroad tracks at Lindale; the house was later owned by Pursley, when it burned. From 1892 Jennie was Weikert Postmaster for about four years. She was listed on White Springs UMC Circuit membership roll as Goodlander. In 1900 census House 15. Thomas was 41, she was 44, James, 15, Jacob, 14, Jeremiah, 7, listed as Eisenhuth. In 1903 she was a Sunday school teacher at Hironimus Church. In 1904 she was Recording Secretary of the Christian Endeavor Society. In 1908 she was a member of the Sunday School Bible Class. In 1910 she was Assistant Secretary of the Sunday School at Hironimus Church.

Children: Rose Louise Goodlander (*b.* 1874, *d.* 1951, *mar.* Albert N. Bitner), John (*b.* 1876, *d.* 1880), James, Jacob, Jeremiah Warren, Daniel Roy Goodlander (*b.* Oct. 7, 1881, *bap.* Dec. 28, 1881, in White Springs UMC Circuit, *mar.* Lottie Keller), Rebecca "Reba" Goodlander (*b.* Oct. 18, 1884, *bap.* May 31, 1885, in White Springs UMC Circuit), possibly also Philip Ray and Benjamin (both *d.* young).
    [F.A.G. 38694784]

MARGARET JANE "JENNIE" TATE
    MRS. AMBROSE DANIEL BETTILYON
b. around 1871/9
d. Jan. 26, 1913/15

bur. Hironimus Union Church Cemetery, Weikert, Union Co, PA
dau. of William Tate and Ellen Tate
mar. Ambrose Daniel Bettilyon, June 21, 1892, White Springs Church, Union Co, PA

Lived at Lindale (Vi Neuhauser's house) on Weikert Road, Weikert. In 1900 census they are listed as tenants.

Children: Amber M. or F., Rhoda E. G. or Rodastella (*d.* at 8 years), George Edward, James C. or Lester (*b.* 1909 in Haines Twsp, Centre Co, PA), Mary E.(?), Jennie (*d.* in childbirth, Jan. 26, 1913), Guy Alvin (adopted out), William O. (*b.* 1898, *d.* 1964, not shown in 1910 census, her name is on his death certificate).

[F.A.G. 99956089]

Jennie Tate Bettilyon
(permission: Bill Cunningham)

BERTHA MAE JOLLY
MRS. GEORGE ALLEN LANDIS
b. June 3, 1894, Lindale, Weikert, Union Co, PA
d. Sept. 24, 1981, Lewisburg, Union Co, PA
bur. Harmony Cemetery, Milton, PA (?)
dau. of Frank Seymour Jolly and Eva Regina Hironimus
mar. George Allen Landis, Aug. 27, 1912.

She was the granddaughter of Allen Jolly and Nancy Jane Zimmerman Jolly and Andrew Hironimus and Lucinda A. Burns Hironimus. He was a railroad pipe fitter and train switchman. For at least ten years they lived in Weikert in a concrete block home probably built by them in 1949. In 1950 they joined Hironimus Union Church. She taught Sunday school in 1950–7.

Children: Clair, Kenneth Franklin, Thelma (*d.* at 12 days).

(permission: Corky Landis)

KATHRYN "KATE" HIRONIMUS
    MRS. JOHN BENJAMIN SHOLTER
b. June 7, 1877, Weikert, Union Co, PA
d. April 9, 1945, Shamokin, Northumberland Co, PA
bur. Old Fellows Cemetery, Shamokin, Northumberland Co, PA
dau. of Andrew Hironimus and Lucy Ann Burns Hironimus
mar. John Benjamin "Shaggy" Sholter, July 7, 1895 or 1896, Weikert

In 1900 census House 39, he was 27, she was 22, Andrew, 4, Ruth, 3; Andrew Derr, 28, lived in household. They moved to Shamokin in 1912–13, where he was a railroad engineer. They had a cabin at Little Mountain Lane, where he died after Kate's death; the property was then sold to Ralph "Scaly" Wagner, then to Don and Jeanne Eckrod.

Children: Andrew, Ruth (*mar.* Kimber C. Farrow), Grace (*mar.* Edward Shawda).

[F.A.G. 153879871]

(permission: Corky Landis)

Women of Weikert

RUTH VIOLA SHOLTER
 MRS. KIMBER C. FARROW
b. Jan. 17, 1897, Hartley Twsp, PA
d. June, 1986, interred July 2, 1986
bur. Doylestown Cemetery, Doylestown, Bucks Co, PA
dau. of John Sholter and Kathryn Hironimus Sholter
mar. Kimber C. Farrow Jr.

Lived on Weikert Road, Weikert, PA. They had the farm across from Hironimus Church. She taught Sunday school at the Hironimus Union Church in 1947–51. She was also an organist at Hironimus Union Church in 1947.

[F.A.G. 61454390]

CORA BELLA MCPHERSON
 MRS. DAVID P. GALER
b. Jan. 15, 1875, Union Co, PA
d. Feb. 26, 1954, Beaver Springs, Snyder Co, PA
bur. Hironimus Union Church Cemetery, Weikert, Union Co, PA
dau. of James Silverwood McPherson and Sarah Catherine Sholter McPherson
mar. David P. Galer, Sept. 1897

1954 Hironimus Union Church Memory List. She may have had a daughter Clara Kline (*b.* 1893) before marriage to Galer.

Children: Charles Newton Galer (*d.* at one year of age), James W., two daughters (*mar.* Hoffman, Klinger).

[F.A.G. 91835567]

Cora B. Galer
(permission:
Bill Cunningham)

IDA C. "BETTY" HIRONIMUS
MRS. LEON HARRISON MILLER
b. Feb. 20, 1898, Lindale, Weikert, Union Co, PA
d. May 20, 1963, Lewisburg, Union Co, or Rock Glen, Luzerne Co, PA
bur. Mountain Grove Cemetery, Luzerne Co, PA
dau. of John William Hironimus and Mary Ellen Freed Hironimus
mar. Leon "Nick" Harrison Miller, 1924

After her marriage she resided in Rock Glen and Holsapple, PA. She was a member of Black Creek Township Methodist Church. According to Budd Hironimus she was a marvelous cook (Hironimus Family Book). In early years she was a Sunday school teacher at Hironimus Union Church.

[F.A.G. 33702720]

(permission: Tim Bastian)

CLARA E. SMITH
MRS. DAVID R. PURSLEY
b. Oct. 25, 1874, Kelly Twsp, Union Co, PA
d. Oct. 29, 1950, Laurelton, Union Co, PA
bur. Hartleton Cemetery, Hartleton, Union Co, PA
dau. of Abram L. Smith and Ellen S. Blyler Smith
mar. David R. "Pete" Pursley, March 9, 1899

In 1917, 1930, 1924 and 1927, she taught Sunday school at Hironimus Union Church. She was a long time member of Laurelton Lutheran Church.

Children (in 1910 census): Helen E. (*mar.* Harter), 9, David N., 8 months.

[F.A.G. 10411148]

Clara Smith
Pursley
(permission:
Jane Ely Foster)

ISABELLE BERTHA JOLLY
   MRS. JONAS WILLIAM BARNET
   MRS. PRESTON B. ALEXANDER
   MRS. LEWIS M. JOHNSON
b. Sept. 17 or 13, 1899, Hartley Twsp, Union Co, PA.
d. April 30, 1985, Orangeville, PA
bur. Hironimus Union Church Cemetery, Weikert, Union Co, PA
dau. of Edward Thomas Jolly and Mary Blanche Bracken Jolly
mar. 1. Jonas William Barnet, Feb. 22, 1921, Lewisburg, PA, *div.* May 31, 1924
mar. 2. Preston B. Alexander, Nov. 17, 1937, Mifflinburg, Union Co, PA
mar. 3. Lewis M. Johnson, Dec. 21, 1963, Millmont, Union Co, PA

In 1903 she was in the Children's Day Program at the Hironimus Union Church. In 1948 she was a Sunday school teacher at the Hironimus Union Church. In 1985 she was on the Memorial list of the Hironimus Union Church.

Children: Edward Earl Barnet (*b.* Jan. 17, 1922, *bap.* White Springs UMC Circuit, April 2, 1922).

[F.A.G. 91828114]

Isabelle Bertha Jolly

MARY E. "MAME" SHOLTER
   MRS. JOHN H. BARNETT
b. Feb. 19, 1881, in PA
d. Feb. 10, 1932
bur. Hironimus Union Church Cemetery, Weikert, Union Co, PA
dau. of William Sholter and Mary Spacht Sholter
mar. John H. Barnett, around 1899

In 1908 Mame (Mayme) was in the Sunday School Bible Class at Hironimus Union Church. In 1900 census House 16, he was 27, she was 19. In 1910 census House 14, he was 36, she was 29, Mabel, 10, Jacob W., 8, Blanche M., 5.

Children: Mable Barnett (*mar.* Kahley: they raised Margaret Lingle), Blanche M., Daisey, Jacob W., Benjamin.

[F.A.G. 91821180]

Mary E.
Barnett
(permission:
Bill Cunningham)

MARGARET ADELE GALER
   MRS. JAMES MCCELLAN HIRONIMUS
b. Sept. 29, 1889, near Pardee, Hartley Twsp, Union Co, PA.
d. Oct. 29/30, 1922
bur. Hironimus Union Church Cemetery, Weikert, Union Co, PA
dau. of Carbon Galer and Cora Spacht Galer Oakes
mar. James McCellan [*sic*] Hironimus, June 29, 1908, Bellefonte

She was raised by her grandparents Amanda C. Derr Spacht and Jacob F. Spacht after her father died when she was two. He was a railroad engineer and logger. In 1908 they moved to Old Town, Maryland, for lumbering work. On Jan. 27, 1911, they returned to Weikert and moved to the Hironimus homestead. They owned 184 acres around Little Mountain.

Children: Mildred Florence (*mar.* Charles William Teichman), Cecil J. (*mar.* Helen E. Arbogast), Argyle E. (*b.* May 7, 1914, *mar.* Marie Flick), Myrtle Rae (*b.* Jan 22, 1916, *mar.* Bruce Schnure), Sarah Anna (*b.* March 18, 1917, *mar.* Marlin Kenee), Hilda (*mar.* James Leasure). Argyle, Myrtle and Sarah *bap.* Aug. 2, 1917, White Springs UMC Circuit.

[F.A.G. 91829109]

Margaret
(permission:
Bill Cunningham)

RUTH MAY HIRONIMUS
MRS. WILLIAM M. PURSLEY
b. April 15, 1900
d. Oct. 22, 1944, Weikert, Union Co, PA
bur. Hironimus Union Church Cemetery, Weikert, Union Co, PA
dau. of John William Hironimus and Mary Ellen Freed Hironimus
mar. William M. Pursley, around 1918

She lived at Lindale, Weikert. In 1903 she was in the Children's Day program at Hironimus Union Church. In 1914–16 she taught Sunday school at Hironimus Union Church. According to Joyce Landis in the "Hironimus Family Tree" book, "Ruth was truly a pioneer woman. Ruth had a baby in the morning and was out splitting wood in the afternoon."

Children: Dorothy Mae (*b.* 1918, *mar.* Neidigh), Minnie Ellen (*mar.* Schreck), Molly (*mar.* Haas), Helen (*mar.* Kinney), Harry S., Elwood E.

[F.A.G. 91825934]

(permission: Tim Bastian)

Martha Harriet "Mamy" McPherson
    Mrs. William McColm
b. Dec. 14, 1839, Ohio
d. Feb. 4, 1914, PA
bur. Hironimus Union Church Cemetery, Weikert, Union Co, PA
dau. of William McPherson and Christiana Moore McPherson
mar. William "Papy" McColm, March 20, 1861, New Berlin, PA

    She and "Papy" raised her niece Clara Clark (mar. Goodlander). In 1900 census they are listed as tenants. She could read but she could not write.
    [F.A.G. 99956132]

Harriet McPherson
(permission:
Bill Cunningham)

Ellen E. Moyer?
    Mrs. William Tate
b. Oct. 4, 1846
d. Dec. 18, 1918, Hartley Twsp, Union Co, PA
mar. William Tate

    Ellen was a sister of Margaret May Moyer (Mrs. Lewis Shaffer). In 1900 census House 153; Margaret Jennie, 26, James, 24, Jamilia, 20, Jennie's husband Ambrose, 29, and granddaughter Mary, 7. In 1910 census William was 61, Ellen, 64, with James, 35, and his wife Margaret, 34.

Children: Annie M. Keister Tate (*b.* May 15, 1871, *bap.* May 8, 1892, White Springs UMC Circuit), James (caretaker of the three "Syndicate Cottages" at Cherry Run, lived in a small shack there).

MARY M. BETTILYON
MRS. BENNETT
b. around 1852 in PA

In 1900 census House 4, living with William A. Longer, widower; he was 43, she was 48, Rose Bennett was 18. In 1910 census House 3, living with William A. Longer.

MARGARET MARY SALOME SPECHT or SPACHT
MRS. WILLIAMS CHARLES SHOLTER
b. March 11, 1857, Middleburg, Snyder Co, PA
d. July 2, 1917, Weikert, Union Co, PA
bur. Hironimus Union Church Cemetery, Weikert, Union Co, PA
dau. of Anthony James Spacht and Mary Ann Webster Spacht
mar. William Charles Sholter, Oct. 6, 1877

He was a railroad repairman and in 1910 a lumberman. Mary was a Sunday school teacher in 1903 and class member in 1908 and 1911–13, in White Springs UMC Circuit. She was also a member of Hironimus Union Church. In 1900 census House 19, he was 46, she was 43, Charles Dervin, 17, Fred, 15, Cora Louise, 12, Jonas, 10. In 1910 census House 21, he was 58, she was 53, Jonas B., 20, a lumberman in the woods.

Children: Anthony James (*b.* June 4, 1879, *bap.* Nov. 29, 1879, White Springs UMC Circuit), Mary Elizabeth (*b.* Feb. 19, 1881, *bap.* July 4, 1881, White Springs UMC Circuit), Charles Dervin (*b.* Aug. 25, 1882, *bap.* July 15, 1883, White Springs UMC Circuit), Fred, Cora Louise (*mar.* Simon Bingaman), Jonas B., Edward.

[F.A.G. 55435544]

Mary S.
(permission:
Bill Cunningham)

ELIZABETH MINERVA BUFFINGTON
  MRS. GEORGE WASHINGTON SHOLTER
b. Nov. 11, 1859, Middleburg, Snyder Co, PA
d. Feb. 1, 1929, Weikert, Union Co, PA
bur. Hironimus Union Church Cemetery, Weikert, Union Co, PA
dau. of Edward Buffington and Amelia Weller Buffington
mar. George Washington Sholter, Oct. 8, 1876, Middleburg, PA

In 1900 census House 24, he was 43, she was 42. She had a beautiful voice and loved to sing hymns.

Children: Carrie C. (*b.* around 1878, *mar. 1.* Herbert Keene, *mar. 2.* Oscar A. Pursley), John E., Edward L. (*b.* around 1884), Asa Roland (*b.* 1887)
  [F.A.G. 99956160]

(permission:
Jerry Sholter,
Tim Bastian)

MARY CATHERINE McPHERSON
  MRS. DAVID C. GALER
b. Oct. 25, 1860, Winfield, Union Co, PA
d. Nov. 7, 1933

bur. Buffalo Church of the Brethren Cemetery, Mifflinburg, Union Co, PA
dau. of James Silverwood McPherson and Sarah C. Sholter McPherson
mar. David C. Galor or Galer, Oct. 30, 1879, Union Co, PA

In 1900 census he was 43, she was 38, Thomas, 13, Harry J., 8, Carrie, 2, Hazel. She was a communicant at the Buffalo Church of the Brethren.

Children (surviving in 1933): John William, Sadie Jane (*mar.* David A. Coup), Elda E. (*mar.* Schumacher), Mrs. Christian Frech, Mrs. Reno M. Hoffman, Arthur.

[F.A.G. 63359265]

(permission: Tony Shively)

NANCY REBECCA HASSINGER
MRS. WILLIAM J. HIRONIMUS
b. Feb. 2, 1863, Centre Co, PA
d. Feb. 5, 1938, Hartley Twsp, at the home of her daughter, Mrs. Daniel Libby
bur. Hironimus Union Church Cemetery, Weikert, Union Co, PA
dau. of O. (or Alfred) P. Hassinger and Rachel A. Strunk Hassinger
mar. William J. Hironimus, Aug. 1887, Union Co, PA

In 1900 census House 11, he was 57, she was 34. In 1910 census House 13, with boarder Jerry Aumiller, 52, lumberman.

Children (in 1900 census): James M., 15, Samuel H. (*b.* Feb. 5, 1888, *bap.* White Springs UMC Circuit), 12, Annie M., 10, William J., 8, Sarah "Sadie" E., 6, Charlotte.

[F.A.G. 88765381]

Nancy R.
(permission:
Bill Cunningham)

PHOEBE A. STYERS
  MRS. KEISTER
  MRS. ZACHARY GALER (?)
b. 1866 or 1869
dau. of Styers and Mary
mar. 1. Keister
mar. ?2. Zachary Galer

In 1870 census Phoebe listed as 4 years old. In 1900 census house 92: Mary Styers, 71, daughter Phoebe, 34, grandson David Keister, 9, grandson Irwin Smith, 1. In 1920 census listed as Styers, 54, married housekeeper; Roland Keister, 29, is a boarder. In 1930 census she is listed as housekeeper and divorced, with Zach Galer, 83, and foster son Clarence. She did pow-wowing when she worked for Mary "Blanche" Jolly. Styers Family Papers, Union County Historical Society has several Phoebe Styers.

Children: David Keister, Edward Galer (*b.* 1904).

ALICE REPPORT
b. around 1867

Lived with S. Kleckner, widower. In 1900 census House 2, he was 45, she was 33, his daughter Susan, 2, Daisy Allen, 15, his brother Richard, 60.

HARRIET CLARA CLARK
  MRS. OSCAR REED GOODLANDER
b. Dec. 21, 1868, in PA
d. July 10, 1956, Harrisburg, Dauphin, Co, PA
bur. Lincoln Chapel Cemetery, Laurelton, Union Co, PA

dau. of Sylvester S. Clark and Jane McPherson Clark (who *d.* 1868–70)
mar. Oscar Reed Goodlander, March 31, 1886, Laurelton, Union Co, PA

Clara was raised by William "Papy" McColm and Harriet "Mamy" McPherson McColm. She was a member of the Women's Auxiliary of the Patriotic Order Sons of America, a member of Daughters of the American Revolution, a member of the Temperance Legion, a member of Hironimus Union Church and in 1907–11 a Sunday school teacher. In 1900 census House 27, he was 31, she was 31. He was listed as a railroad engineer. She raised ten children on the farm near the church. According to August "Pop" Barnett she was known as a very dedicated Christian.

Children (in 1900 census): Bertha, 13 (*mar.* James Bilger), Bessie H(elen), 10 (*mar.* Lundgren), John Leroy (or Lenhart), 7, Benjamin T., 4, Albert Newton Bitner, 2, William McColm, Harriet (*mar.* Snyder).

[F.A.G. 38695069]

H. Clara Goodlander
daughter of S. S. and Jane
McPherson Clark
(permission:
Sandy Vandertol)

ANNIE S. (BRUSS)
MRS. JOHN CHARLES BRUSS
b. 1870
d. 1932
bur. St. Peter's Church Cemetery, Hartleton, Union Co, PA
mar. John Charles Bruss

In 1900 census House 22, she and Charles are listed as tenants, between Ed Jolly and Benjamin Sholter. He was 37, she was 31.

Children (in 1900 census): Mary, 11, Elmer Isaac, 9, Oscar F., 7, Abraham, 5, Clarence D., 2 (*d.* 1902 age 4, *bur.* Keister Cemetery), Kate, 3 months.

[F.A.G. 125546360]

LILY E. JORDAN
MRS. WILLIAM FRANKLIN BARNET
b. Jan. 15, 1870, Buffalo Twsp, Union Co, PA
d. Jan. 1, 1923
bur. Hironimus Union Church Cemetery, Weikert, Union Co, PA
dau. of Richard Jordan and Sarah Jordan
mar. William Franklin Barnet, Dec. 25, 1899, Watsontown, PA

Lillie B., Lillian Bell, Lillie E. William was born in Union County and a resident of Weikert. In 1900 census they were listed as tenants; he was 20 and she was 20. In 1904 she was Treasurer of the Christian Endeavor Society, Hironimus Union Church. In 1908 she was a member of the Sunday School Bible Class, Hironimus Union Church. She was also superintendent of the Cradle Roll Department. House 15 in 1910 census. In 1911–12 and 1916–17 she was a Sunday school teacher at Hironimus Union Church.

Children: Jonas W., Dora Jane (d. 1912, age 6 yrs.)
[F.A.G. 91832224]

Lillie B.
(permission: Bill Cunningham)

ANNIE MINERVA KLECKNER
MRS. GEORGE BURNS HIRONIMUS
b. Sept. 12, 1872 or 1874, Hartley Twsp, Union Co, PA
d. March 15, 1918, East Buffalo Twsp, Union Co, PA
bur. Hironimus Union Church Cemetery, Weikert, Union Co, PA
dau. of Lewis Kleckner and Rachel (Feese or Freas) Kleckner
mar. George Burns Hironimus, June 11, 1893

In 1900 census House 13, he was 30, she was 27, Mabel Emma, 3. In

1910 census House 8, he was 40, she was 38; David Benny was a boarder.

Children: Mabel Emma (*b.* Feb. 13, 1897, *bap.* June 12, 1897, White Springs UMC Circuit), Eva May, George F., Laura K.

[F.A.G. 91829738]

Annie Kleckner Hironimus
(permission: Bill Cunningham)

MARY ELLEN (ELLEN M., ELLA M.) FREED
MRS. JOHN WILLIAM HIRONIMUS
b. Feb. 22, 1873, Union Co, PA
d. May 10, 1930, Hartley Twsp, Union Co, PA.
bur. Hironimus Union Church Cemetery, Weikert, Union Co, PA
dau. of Theodore Freed and Selena Isabelle Corbin Freed
mar. John William Hironimus, around 1889

He was a railroad laborer and a great lumberman. In 1900 census House 14 (as Ellen). He was 34, she was 27. In 1910 census House 9. 1930 Letters Testamentary 1900–1999 Union County Courthouse.

Children: Bessie M. (*b.* 1890, *mar.* Ammon Shaffer), Albert Valentine, Charles F. (*b.* 1894, *mar.* Amelia Jones), Lucy B. (*b.* 1895, *mar.* Roy Custer), Ida C. (*b.* 1898, *mar.* Leon Miller), Ruth May (*b.* 1900, *mar.* William Pursley), Guy R. (*b.* 1902, *mar.* 1. Florence Savage, *mar.* 2. Catherine), Mark E. (*b.* 1905, *mar.* Odessa Watkins), John W. (*b.* 1907, *mar.* Mabel Jones), Mildred Rose (*b.* 1909, *mar.* Henry Benson), twins Luke and Geraldine (*d.* at birth).

[F.A.G. 91827974]

Mary E.
(permission: Bill Cunningham)

SARA (GALER)
   MRS. DAVID GALER
b. around 1875
mar. David Galer
   In 1900 census House 37, he was 24, she was 25.
   Children (in 1900 census), James, 2, Charles, 1; Clara Kline, 7, may have been her daughter.

LILLIAN J. (JOHNSON)
   MRS. WILLIAM JOHNSON
b. Dec. 24, 1876
d. May 15, 1944
bur. Hironimus Union Church Cemetery, Weikert, Union Co, PA
mar. William Johnson
   In 1900 census House 5. He is 30, she is 24.
   Children: Jennie, William
   [F.A.G. 91835822]

Lillian J. Johnson
(permission: Bill Cunningham)

ISABELL ANN AUMILLER
   MRS. SAMUEL CONRAD WILT
b. March 4, 1878, Union Co, PA
d. May 29, 1913, Lewistown, Mifflin Co, PA
bur. Hironimus Union Church Cemetery, Weikert, Union Co, PA
dau. of Manassah T. Aumiller and Sarah Agnes Badger Aumiller
mar. Samuel Conrad "Junior" Wilt, July 29, 1894
   In 1900 census House 3. He was 26, she was 24. Their house burned and they later lived in Milroy.
   Children (in 1900 census): Mary Ann, 4, Bessie Agnes, 3, Lee David, 2,

Walter Clarence, Samuel, Mildred "Tillie," Grace Dora.
[F.A.G. 88755230]

Isabell wife of
S. C. Wilt
(permission:
Bill Cunningham)

EVA REGINA HIRONIMUS
MRS. FRANK SEYMORE JOLLY
b. Dec. 26, 1872 or 1873, Union Co, PA
d. Sept. 6, 1946, Milton, Northumberland Co, PA
bur. Harmony Cemetery, Milton, Northumberland Co, PA
dau. of Andrew Hironimus and Lucy Burns Hironimus
mar. Frank Seymore Jolly, March 20, 1891

She was a member of the First Evangelical Church, Milton, PA. He was listed as railroad laborer, railroad agent at Lindale, and Pennsylvania Railroad inspector. In 1900 census House 8, he was 31, she was 26, Bertha Mae, 5, Charles Allen, 3.

Children: Arthur (*b.* and *d.* 1892), Bertha Mae, Charles Allen (*b.* Jan. 14, 1897, *bap.* June 1897, White Springs UMC Circuit), Florence, Clair F., Martha L.

(permission:
Corky Landis)

Mary Blanche Bracken
Mrs. Edward Thomas Jolly

b. Sept. 21, 1876, Belsano, Black Lick Twsp, Cambria Co, PA
d. March 8, 1964, Millmont, Union Co, PA
bur. Hironimus Union Church Cemetery, Weikert, Union Co, PA
dau. of John or Davis Bracken and Belle Bracken
mar. Edward Thomas Jolly, Aug. 3, 1898, Ebensburg, Cambria Co, PA

They lived on Jolly's Grove Lane, Weikert, PA. In 1900 census House 21, listed as Blanche. He was 26, she was 22, Isabella, 9 months. In 1907 she built the farm house on the town side of Penns Creek with $750 she made from boarding hunters and fishermen. In 1908 she was a member of the Hironimus Union Church Sunday School Bible Class and a Sunday school teacher. On Nov. 5, 1909, she bought for $375 approximately 26 acres along the creek and the railroad from Henry and Hannah Dorman. On Oct. 1, 1924 or 1925, she bought for $90 a lot of 100 ft. along the creek from Joseph J. and Dorothy C. Augustine and William and Olga Henn. Mary and Edward ran Jolly's Grove Campground. She gave "taffy pull" parties for the neighborhood girls. She was describe as a "dear." She played mouth organ and she was noted for her artwork.

Children: Isabella (Isabelle), Hilda, Clarence Dale (*d.* Jan. 4, 1915, of gunshot wounds to the leg, age 13).

[F.A.G. 91836095]

(permission: Mary Ann Losick)

Amber Mae Bettilyon
Mrs. Jacob Charles Barnett

b. March 28, 1903 or 1904, in PA
d. June 10, 1927 or 1928, Hamburg Sanitorium, Berks Co, PA, of tuberculosis.

bur. Hironimus Union Church Cemetery, Weikert, Union Co, PA
dau. of Ambrose Daniel Bettilyon and Margaret Jane "Jennie" Foltz (Tate)
mar. Jacob Charles Barnett

She was listed as a participant in the Children's Day Program at Hironimus Union Church.

Children: William D. Barnett, Irene M. Barnett (*mar.* Hill), or were they children of Jake's second wife Blanche?

[F.A.G. 91821122]

Amber M. Barnett
(permission:
Gerri Aitken)

JESSIE HELEN BICKEL
  MRS. AUGUST KARL BAUER
b. May 8, 1897, Philadelphia (according to the Philadelphia Social Security Register)
d. May 22, 1983, Lewisburg, Union Co, PA
dau. of George Washington Bickel and Jessie Pardoe Bickel
mar. August Karl Bauer, Sept. 17, 1921

Helen came to the area as a child with her grandparents. Her family rented in Weikert in the summers. After World War II, Helen and her own family once again spent summers in Weikert. They bought "Nahanne" on the creek as their 16-year retirement home. Helen was small in stature but large in spirit. According to her daughter-in-law Irene Bauer she was a great cook and excellent correspondent. She was a graduate of Girls High, Philadelphia. She had an M.Ed. From the University of Pennsylvania and taught school for many years. She compiled "The Story of the Hironimus Union Church" in 1970. The family was great friends with the Sholter and Wirt families and traveled overseas with Leona Sholter Wirt and Ben Wirt. Her remains were scattered along with those of her husband on Jack's Mountain.

Children: James A., L. George, Richard C., Robert E.

(permission: Irene Bauer)

VIRGINIA GERTRUDE LIBBY
  MRS. JONAS WILLIAM BARNETT
  MRS. JAMES LESTER BETTILYON
b. Nov. 29, 1906, Weikert, Union Co, PA
d. Oct. 30, 1989, Lewisburg, Union Co, PA
bur. Hironimus Union Church Cemetery, Weikert, Union Co, PA
dau. of Daniel Carey Libby Sr. and Ida Seymour Freed Libby
mar. 1. James William Barnett, July 20, 1925, White Springs Church, Union Co, PA
mar. 2. James Lester Bettilyon, Feb 13, 1937, at Millmont, Union Co, PA
  Hironimus Church member.
  Children: L. Jane Barnett (*mar.* Strickler), Jonas Franklin, Cora "Toady," August "Pop," Barbara Bettilyon, Ida Geraldine, Lester.
  [F.A.G. 91820915]

(compiler's collection)

MRS. ANN BARKER
  In 1908 she was a member of the Sunday School Bible Class at Hironimus Union Church.

Maud or Maude Johnson

b. May 20, 1882, Weikert, Union Co, PA
d. 1954
bur. Long Lane Cemetery, Laurelton, Union Co, PA
dau. of David Crawford Johnson and Hannah Mary Weikel Johnson

In 1903 she was a Sunday school teacher at Hironimus Union Church. In 1904 she was Corresponding Secretary of the Christian Endeavor Society, Hironimus Union Church. She was a member of the Sunday School Bible Class in 1908 and Secretary of the class in 1909. In 1914 she was organist at the Hironimus Union Church.

[F.A.G. 122080590]

Maud Johnson
(permission: Jane Ely Foster)

Hilda May Jolly

b. July 6, 1903
d. July 2, 1981
bur. Hironimus Union Church Cemetery, Weikert, Union Co, PA
dau. of Edward Thomas Jolly and Mary Blanche Bracken Jolly

Lived on Jolly's Grove Lane, Weikert, PA. In 1903 she was mentioned in Children's Day Program of Hironimus Union Church. In 1950 she was Parole officer at Laurelton State Village. In 1966 she retired as Director of Social Services after 44½ years of service. She was a member of the Pennsylvania Business Women's Association and a member of Sacred Heart Roman Catholic Church in Lewisburg. She traveled much in her job and had also directed dramatics.

[F.A.G. 99956122]

Hilda May Jolly

Cora Catherine Barker
    Mrs. William W. Koonsman
b. Sept. 25, 1875, Centre Co, PA
d. June 21, 1943, Lewis Twsp, Union Co, PA
bur. Old Cedars Cemetery, Swengel, Union Co, PA
dau. of Frank P. Barker and Sarah E. Schultz Barker
mar. William W. Koonsman, around 1892

He was listed as railroad repair laborer. The family rented from John Barnett. In 1903 the Koonsmans were in Centre Co, PA. In 1909, 1911 and 1914 she was a Sunday school teacher at Hironimus Union Church. In 1910 census House 12, he was 38, she was 35.

Children (in 1910 census): Lottie Elizabeth (*mar.* Chester Rea Fox, April 19, 1915), 14, Franklin C., 12, Reba C. (*mar.* Charles E. Wenrich), 9, Ray Reynolds, 6.

[F.A.G. 12511 3009]

Susan Alice Irwin
    Mrs. Arthur J. Kreps
b. Feb. 9, 1903, Weikert, Union Co, PA
d. April 11, 1979, Weikert, Union Co, PA
bur. Lincoln Chapel Cemetery, Laurelton, Union Co, PA
dau. of John Irwin and Charlotte Hironimus Irwin
mar. Arthur J. Kreps, March 31, 1921, Laurelton, PA

Lived at Lindale. Before that they had the Pursley home. She gave a piano to the church and was a quilter and crafter. In 1979 she was remembered in the Hironimus Union Church Memory List.

CORA E. LIBBY
MRS. JAMES GARRETSON PRICE
b. July 9 or 19, 1909, Weikert, Union Co, PA
d. March 29, 2003
bur. Hironimus Union Church Cemetery, Weikert, Union Co, PA
dau. of Daniel Carey Libby and Ida Seymour Freed Libby
mar. James Garretson Price, June 7, 1929, Milton, PA

Lived in Joe Sholter's old house behind the store before moving to Mifflinburg. Worked at Laurelton State Village. In 1924–5 and 1948 taught Sunday school at Hironimus Union Church.

Children: Carey G., Thomas F., William L. "Bo," Rosemary P., J. Travers. [F.A.G. 91828402]

Cora E. Price
(permission:
Bill Cunningham)

CHARLOTTE MAY "LOTTIE" HIRONIMUS
MRS. JOHN E. IRWIN
MRS. GEORGE LINCOLN ZECHMAN
b. Dec. 27, 1882, Weikert, Hartley Twsp, Union Co, PA
d. May 24, 1967, Lewisburg, Union Co, PA
bur. Long Lane Cemetery, Laurelton, Union Co, PA
dau. of Andrew Hironimus and Lucy Burns Hironimus
mar. 1. John E. Irwin, Nov. 28, 1899, Hartleton, Hartley Twsp, Union Co, PA
mar. 2. George Lincoln Zechman

Lived at Lindale in original Hironimus home behind Harold Klauger's and Roy Ott's places; the foundation is still there. She was a member of Hironimus Union Church and then Pleasant Grove Union Church.

Children (by John Irwin): Susan Alice (b. 1903, mar. Arthur J. Kreps), Kathryn E. (mar. Gordon G. Fritz), Pauline L. (mar. Ely), Esther W. (mar. Shipper), Therlow B., John L.

(permission: Corky Landis)

Helen Elizabeth Neuhauser
  Mrs William Earl Ammon
b. 1908
d. 1994
bur. Bellevue Presbyterian Cemetery, Gap, Lancaster Co, PA
dau. of Joseph and Elizabeth Stoltzfus Neuhauser
mar. William Earl Ammon (*b.* 1905, *d.* 1950)

She owned "The Tin Shanty" on White Mountain Road, later in the hands of her daughter Betsy L. Kell. Then she lived in the big house "Pine Acres," now "Walnut Hill Farm" next to the Weikert Store, with her sisters Sadie C. Neuhauser and Mary S. Neuhauser. They sold to Levans in about 1973 and moved to Bethlehem, PA. She had worked at Laurelton Village.

[F.A.G. 77569796]

(permission: Betsy Kell)

Sarah Agnes Badger
Mrs. Manassah T. Aumiller

b. Nov. 8, 1863, or Jan. 1862
d. July 5, 1952
bur. Hironimus Union Church Cemetery, Weikert, Union Co, PA
dau. of Bob Badger
mar. Manassah T. Aumiller

In 1883 they were in Lindale, where Mary N. was born. In 1897 she owned 19 perches near William Johnson and Penns Creek. In 1910 census House 5, he was 52, she was 49. In 1952 she is on Hironimus Union Church Memory List.

Children: Williamson Washington "Sawmiller" Aumiller (*b.* 1878), Cleveland Manassah (*b.* 1888), Mary Normatta (*mar.* Cherry), Isabell (*mar.* Wilt).

[F.A.G. 74041795]

Sarah A. Aumiller (permission: Curtis Stroup)

Harriet "Hattie" Susanna Bogar
Mrs. Robert Franklin Bilger

b. March 6 or 16, 1858
d. May 11, 1930
bur. Long Lane Cemetery, Union Co, PA
dau. of Daniel J. Bogar and Susanna Sampsell Bogar
mar. Robert Franklin Bilger, Snyder Co, PA

Lived on Weikert Road, Weikert, Union Co, PA. In 1910 census he is 53, she is 52 (sons George, 18, Paul, 14). In 1917 and 1919 her name is on mineral rights agreements with George H. Smull. In 1917 her husband had a car and was listed as being in Glen Iron. Her granddaughter, Caroline Bilger Wenrick, was born at Harriet's home, May 11, 1917.

Children: George W., Maudella, Paul, Charles (?), Mary "Mame," Carrie, James D., Lottie (?).

[F.A.G. 122080449]

(permission: Caroline Wenrick)

ARAMINDI "RINDY" BETTLYON
  Lived at 7715 Weikert Rd., Weikert, PA.
  Children: Ambrose Bettilyon (she lived with Alvah Longer around 1910/20 and was buried at Pleasant Grove UMC Cemetery, Union Co, PA).
  [F.A.G. 99956090]

MARY NORMATTA AUMILLER
  MRS. DANIEL CHERRY
b. Jan. 22, 1883, Union Co, PA
d. May 15, 1910, Lindale, Union Co, PA
bur. Hironimus Union Church Cemetery, Weikert, Union Co, PA
dau. of Manassah T. Aumiller and Sarah Agnes Badger Aumiller
mar. Daniel Cherry, 1905
  In 1910 census House 4. He is 26, she is 25.
  Children: Morrison (or Morgan) Darlington (*b.* 1906, Reedsville), Charles E. (*b.* 1908). She died 5 days after baby boy Leroy was born and he died 3 months later.
  [F.A.G. 99956099]

Mary N. wife of
Daniel Cherry
(permission:
Bill Cunningham)

ESTELLA ELIZABETH REPPERT
  MRS. ELMER RENO DAUBERMAN
b. Sept. 25, 1891/2
d. Aug. 10, 1974, Lewisburg, Union Co, PA
bur. Hironimus Union Church Cemetery, Weikert, Union Co, PA
dau. of John E. Rheppard and Mary Jane "Jennie" Aumiller Boop Rheppard
mar. Elmer Reno Dauberman
  He was a farm laborer.
  Children: Dorothy Jane (*b.* Sept. 8, 1910, *bap.* April 2, 1922, in the White Springs UMC Circuit, *mar.* Good), Clair (*mar.* Clifford), Gerald L., Olive Mae, Arthur C. "Bud," P. Jean, John R., Betty
  [F.A.G. 91826305]

Estella E.
Daubermann
(permission:
Bill Cunningham)

HANNAH (JOHNSON)
  MRS. WILLIAM JOHNSON
b. around 1853
mar. William Johnson (whose father was *b.* in Canada)
  In 1910 census House 1, he was 66, she was 57.
  Children (in 1910 census): Carrie, 34, Clayton, 22.

MARY ETTA ELY
   MRS. DAVID CRAWFORD JOHNSON
b. May 21, 1875, Hartley Twsp, Union Co, PA
d. Jan. 24, 1968, Union Co, PA
bur. Long Lane Cemetery, Laurelton, Union Co, PA
dau. of David Ely and Catherine Nearhood Ely
mar. David Crawford Johnson, May 23, 1911

She was a schoolteacher. She married David fifteen years after his first wife, Hannah Mary Weikel, died. She served as a sewing instructor at Laurelton State School and Hospital. In 1920–3 she was a Sunday school teacher at Hironimus Union Church. In 1968 she was remembered on the Hironimus Union Church Memory List.

Children: Walter C. Johnson (*b.* 1912).
[F.A.G. 76842625]

circa 1907
(permission:
Jane Ely Foster)

MABEL IRENE BARNET
   MRS. ELMER ELSWORTH KAHLEY
b. Aug. 31, 1899
d. July 7, 1971, Lewisburg Union Co, PA
bur. Hironimus Union Church Cemetery, Weikert, Union Co, PA
dau. of John H. Barnet and Mary Sholter Barnet
mar. Elmer Elsworth Kahley, Sept. 2 or 11, 1915, Laurelton, PA

In 1913 and 1934 she was a Sunday school teacher at Hironimus Union Church. In 1971 she was remembered on the Hironimus Union Church Memory Roll. She was known for her delicious pies, which her two boys sold from a wagon for 25c each.

Children: Carl E., Eugene F., Lois (*mar.* Sullenberger or Schellenberger), John Jay (*b.* Nov. 10, 1916, *bap.* Sept. 27, 1917, White Springs UMC Circuit), Jenny Virginia.
[F.A.G. 91836277]

(permission: Kitty Frederick)

TOME ELVERTA HOSTERMAN
MRS. JOHN CALVIN KRUMRINE
b. April 15, 1876, Haines Twsp, Centre Co, PA
d. Jan. 10, 1941, Danville State Hospital, Montour Co, PA
bur. Union Cemetery, Woodward, Centre Co, PA
dau. of Thomas William Hosterman and Rachel Vonada Hosterman
mar. John C. Krumrine (*b.* 1874, *d.* 1934)

In 1930 census Owen E. "Hap" Everett, 25, was their hired man. They owned the farm where the Union County Sportsmen's Club is now. Her family is written up in Jordan, *Genealogical and Personal History of Northern Pennsylvania*, I, 112-13.
[F.A.G. 167889275]

(compiler's collection)

SADIE C. NEUHAUSER
b. 1897
d. 1984
bur. Bellevue Presbyterian Cemetery, Gap, Lancaster Co, PA
dau. of Joseph Neuhauser and Elizabeth Stoltzfus Neuhauser

She lived in the big house ("Pine Acres," now "Walnut Hill Farm") next to the Weikert store with her sisters Mary S. Neuhauser and Helen W. Ammon. They sold to the Levans around 1973 and moved to Bethlehem, PA. Sadie was employed for a time at the Laurelton State School.

[F.A.G. 77504327]

(permission: Seth Neuhauser)

ELIZABETH M. SNYDER SHAFFER
    MRS. VICTOR NEUHAUSER
b. April 20, 1912, Weikert, Union Co, PA
d. Jan. 31, 1931, Weikert, Union Co, PA
bur. Hironimus Union Church Cemetery, Weikert, Union Co, PA
dau. of Ammon John Shaffer and Bess Hironimus Shaffer
mar. Victor Neuhauser, around 1929

Lived on Weikert Road. Died just after childbirth. In 1924–6 and 1928 she taught Sunday school at Hironimus Union Church. Remembered in Hironimus Cradle Roll.

    Children: Samuel (*d.* at 2 days)

[F.A.G. 91848007]

Elizabeth wife of
Victor Neuhauser
(permission:
Bill Cunningham)

N.... KNOBLE
    MRS. GEORGE OBERLE
    She was still living in May 1918. Lived on north side of Weikert Road near first railroad crossing. Rented or owned Camp Lindale. From Philadelphia and returned to Philadelphia.
    Children: George, Hilda.

MARGARET "MAGGIE" MOYER
    MRS. LEWIS SHAFFER
    b. April 13, 1849, Hartley Twsp, Union Co, PA
    d. March 24, 1916
    bur. Hironimus Union Church Cemetery, Weikert, Union Co, PA
    dau. of William Moyer and N... Goodlander Moyer
    mar. Lewis Shaffer, around 1868
    Margaret was a sister of Mrs. William Tate. Known also as "Auntie Maggie May." In 1910 census House 10, in Lindale. He was 57, she was 47. In 1899–1909 she taught young ladies and Sunday school at Hironimus Union Church, where she was a member.
    Children: Rachel Jane (*d.* July 5, 1882, at age 12).
    [F.A.G. 14548426? in Union Co]

CLARA E. BARTLEY
    MRS. EDWARD L. SHOLTER
    b. June 17, 1884, Laurelton, Union Co, PA
    d. Dec. 20, 1957, Harrisburg, Dauphin Co, PA
    bur. Dauphin Cemetery, Dauphin Co, PA
    dau. of Henry Bartley and Mary Styers Bartley
    mar. Edward L. Sholter, Jan 24., 1901, Union Co, PA
    He was a lumberman then railroad car repairman. In 1910 census House

20, he was 25, she was 25, Rosella H., 8, Guy. 7. In 1910 she was organist at Hironimus Union Church. By 1920 living in Dauphin borough. She died of bronchial pneumonia.

Children: Dorothy, Janet, Rosella, Guy, Ellsworth, Edna M. (age 7 in 1920).

[F.A.G. 159832557]

(permission: Tim Bastian)

VERNA THEORA ERDLEY
   MRS. ASA ROLAND SHOLTER
b. Jan. 31, 1890, Middleburg/Swineford, Snyder Co, PA
d. April 1982, Sunbury, Northumberland Co, PA
bur. Hironimus Union Church Cemetery, Weikert, Union Co, PA
dau. of Jerome Erdley and Lillian Reitz Erdley
mar. Asa "Ace" Roland Sholter, May 28, 1910, Lewisburg, Union Co, PA

She was from the Middleburg area of Snyder Co. She was a member of the Hironimus Union Church and taught Sunday school in 1911, 1916, 1919–48, 1957. They donated paint for the Hironimus Union Church to be painted in 1959.

Children: Leona Lillian (*mar.* Wirt), George J., Joseph R.
[F.A.G. 99956151]

(permission: Tim Bastian, Jerry Sholter)

AMBER M. GOODLANDER
b. April 4, 1916
d. April 30, 2007, Lewisburg, Union Co, PA.
bur. Hironimus Union Church Cemetery, Weikert, Union Co, PA

RUTH ANN WILSON
  MRS. GEORGE WILLIAM BILGER
b. Feb. 9, 1889, Huntingdon Co, PA (Feb. 19, 1890, PA death certificate)
d. May 9, 1940 (May 10, 1940, PA death certificate)
bur. Long Lane Cemetery, Laurelton, Union Co, PA
dau. of William Benner Wilson and Caroline Starr
mar. George William Bilger, June 26, 1913, Three Springs, Huntingdon Co, PA

Her family dates back to Philip Benner of Centre County and "Rock."

Children: Laura (*mar.* E. Kauffman Rishel), Lottie (*mar.* Brown), Pauline (*mar.* Thompson), June "Betty" (*mar.* Tyson), Caroline (*mar.* Wenrick), George H., Wilson E. "Gene." Also William Benner and John, both *d.* around age one year.

[F.A.G. 122080449]

(permission: Forrest Wenrick)

BLANCHE PURSLEY
MRS. JACOB CHARLES BARNETT
bur. Hironimus Union Cemetery (tombstone with Amber Barnett?)
mar. Jacob Charles Barnett, his second wife.
Children: Irene Mary (*mar.* Hill?), William (*b.* Feb. 17, 1921)

MARGARETTA KATHRYN GEYER
MRS. JACOB CHARLES BARNETT
b. June 9, 1905, New Columbia, Union Co, PA
d. July 6, 1998, Lewisburg, Union Co, PA
bur. Hironimus Union Church Cemetery, Weikert, Union Co, PA
dau. of Edward Geyer and Hester Kuhns Geyer
mar. Jacob Charles Barnett, after 1923

Lived on Barnett Road, Weikert. Jake married previously Amber, Blanche, and Edna Mae Middlesworth (*div.* Aug. 1933). In 1934 Kathryn taught Sunday School at Hironimus Union Church. She was an attendant at Laurelton Center.

She had two step-children, William D. Barnett and Irene M. Hill. Her only child was Freda Joyce Barnett Barker, *b.* March 11, 1946, now of State College, PA.

[F.A.G. 99956088]

(permission: Eugene Kahley)

Vada P. Dorman
 Mrs. Miles D. Erdley
b. 1921, Hartleton, Union Co, PA
d. Dec. 14, 1994
bur. Hartleton Cemetery, Union Co, PA
mar. Miles D. Erdley, in 1942 (*b.* 1907, *d.* 1965, *bur.* Hartleton)
 She was Thomas Libby's maid.
 Children: She had Mary Lou Sholter (*b.* April 17, 1939) with George J. Sholter before marriage to Miles D. Erdley (brother of Verna Theora Erdley). She had Ruth Denise Erdley (*bap.* Nov. 5, 1942, according to *Mifflinburg Telegraph*) and Eunice M. Erdley (*b.* 1943, Millmont, *d.* Aug. 8, 2014, *mar.* Richard Swain).
 [F.A.G. 10410667]

Anna Minerva Weller
 Mrs. Harry Jefferson Greene
b. Nov. 5, 1880 or 1888, near Laurelton, Union Co, PA
d. Dec. 6, 1963, Lewisburg, Union Co, PA
bur. Highland Cemetery, New Columbia, Union Co, PA
dau. of Daniel O. Weller and Mary Adela Jolly Weller
mar. Harry Jefferson Greene, his second wife
 She was a 20-year resident of Weikert. In 1940 they were renters in House 15 in Hartley Twsp. He was in road construction. Around 1943 they moved from Weikert to Milton. (He died Nov. 5, 1944, in Danville.) She was a member of St. Peter's Evangelical United Brethren Church of Milton.

Children: June, Harold, Joyce—listed as having been born in Scranton, PA, between 1927 and 1932.

[F.A.G. 168013636]

ETHEL BORDER
MRS. ELMER J. KEISTER
mar. Elmer J. Keister

In Millerstown, Perry Co, in 1919; in Weikert in 1922.

Children: Florence (*mar.* Stamm), Helen (*mar.* Poeth), Harry Paul (*b.* 1919, *bur.* Lewisburg Cemetery), Earl (*b.* 1922).

KATHARINA "KATE" (REICH, KORTEN)
MRS. REICH
MRS. AUGUST KORTEN
b. 1872
d. 1936
bur. Hironimus Union Church Cemetery, Weikert, Union Co, PA
mar. 1. Reich (who committed suicide)
mar. 2. August "Pop" Korten (a widower)

He came to Sunbury in 1902. In 1904 he was President of the Sunbury German Club. In 1913 he was Assistant Superintendent of the Susquehanna Silk Mill. In 1925 the Kortens bought "Avian Haven"—8035 Weikert Road, Weikert—with about 186 acres from George Bilgers. Kate was supposedly the first woman to shoot a deer in that area.

Children from first marriage: N..., Herman Frederick.

[F.A.G. 99956144]

Katharina
Reich Korten
(permission:
Bill Cunningham)

Women of Weikert

SARAH E. HIRONIMUS
   MRS. DANIEL CARY LIBBY
b. May 2, 1894
d. March 7, 1986
bur. Juniata Memorial Cemetery, Lewistown, Mifflin Co, PA
dau. of William Hironimus Sr. and Nancy Rebecca Hassinger Hironimus
mar. Daniel Cary Libby Jr.

In 1927–8 she taught Sunday school at Hironimus Union Church. She later lived in Reedsville, Mifflin Co, PA.

Children: Marjorie M. (*mar.* Shively), Katherine Virginia (*mar. 1.* Shaw, *mar. 2.* Martin), Roger, Josephine E. (*mar.* Mayes), Lyman, Nancy (*mar.* Ney), Jean L. (*mar.* Boyer), Harold, Ethel R. (*mar.* Caldwell), Marion S. (*mar.* Prior/Priar), Ralph T., Paul William, Jack S., Donald Roger.

[F.A.G. 45472297]

circa 1913
(permission: Wirt/Boop)

MARY A. (MORGAN)
   MRS. ROBERT S. MORGAN
b. 1863 or 1866
d. 1944
mar. Robert S. Morgan

Probably not long time residents of Weikert. In 1920 census "lodgers" with the Galbraith family in Milton. In 1930 census House 19 in Weikert. He was 69, she was 64. They lived between William Barnett and Ammon Shaffer. He was born around 1861 in Wales and was a machinist. He died in Hartley Township on July 6, 1933, and was buried in Watsontown. In 1940

census House 31, a Mary R. Morgan, 75, widow.
[F.A.G. 162050260?]

Janet Edberg
   Mrs. George J. Sholter
b. Sept. 13, 1923
d. Oct. 30, 1992
bur. Lakeview Cemetery, Jamestown, Chatauqua Co, New York
dau. of Evald G. Edberg and Hazel Munson Edberg
mar. George J. Sholter Sr.

Janet attended Mifflinburg High School and was President of the Home Economics Club. She was an organist at Hironimus Union Church and taught Sunday school.

Children: Beverly.
[F.A.G. 11765055]

Mabel McCloskey
   Mrs. Arthur C. Silvius
b. around 1886, Austin, Potter Co, PA
d. 1936
mar. Arthur C. Silvius, around 1911

He was a Pennsylvania State Forester and in 1918 designed the Hairy John State Park Picnic Area. They were renters between Krumrine's and George and Elizabeth Sholter. He was *bur.* Charles Baber Cemetery, Pottsville, Schuylkill Co, in 1955; spouse was then Susan H.

Children (in 1920 census): Miriam R. (*mar.* Briggman), 7.

Annie (Skyler)
b. around 1867

In 1920 census she was a widow, 53, and housekeeper in household of William Charles Sholter, 68. He was a home owner living next to William F. and Lillie E. Barnet. His wife Mary Specht Sholter *d.* 1917. In 1930 he was living alone on Cherry Run Road and *d.* 1939.

Carrie Mae Snyder
   Mrs. William Reynolds Valentine
b. March 3, 1876, Pleasant Grove, Lewis Twsp, Union Co, PA
d. Feb. 21, 1943, Hartley Twsp, Union Co, PA

bur. East Side Cemetery, Mifflinburg, Union Co, PA
dau. of John Wesley Snyder and Agnes Sophia Acker Snyder
mar. William Reynolds "Billy" Valentine, Oct. 13, 1898, Hartleton, PA

Lived on Weikert Road near Ely's; house was torn down in 1968. Owned farm with Carrie's brother Charles Snyder, who lived in Norristown. In 1900 they lived in East Buffalo Township, and in 1910 in Old Town, Maryland, then Weikert in the 1920s. They boarded hunters. In 1927 she was a Sunday school teacher and organist at Hironimus Union Church. They had no children but helped to rear nephew Kenneth Ely and niece Virginia "Jean" Ely (*mar.* Schneeberg).

[F.A.G. 129537831]

circa 1942
(permission:
Jane Ely Foster)

LEONA LILLIAN ELIZABETH SHOLTER
MRS. BENJAMIN H. WIRT
b. Dec. 12, 1911, Weikert, Union Co, PA
d. Feb. 12, 2013, Lewisburg, Union Co, PA
bur. Hironimus Union Church Cemetery, Weikert, Union Co, PA
dau. of Asa Roland "Ace" Sholter and Verna Theora Erdley Sholter
mar. Benjamin H. Wirt, Dec. 30, 1931, Frederick, Maryland

Lived at 5536 Weikert Road, Weikert, and in Sunbury, PA. She voted in every election for 77 years. She graduated from Hartley Township High School, Laurelton, in 1929. In 1920–8 and 1947–68 she taught Sunday school at Hironimus Union Church and was one of the last teachers when the Sunday school was closed in 1968. She was named to the Hironimus Union Church Council of Elders in 1997. (See *Millmont Times*, vol. 12, no. 8, Dec. 1, 2011.)

Children: Connie (*b.* Oct. 24, 1936, *mar.* Bastian), Francis (*b.* 1938).
[F.A.G. 99956172]

(permission: Tim Bastian)

Marguerite Cressinger
    Mrs. Robert B. Bilger
b. Oct. 12, 1916, Sunbury
d. May 16, 2012, Winter Haven, Florida
bur. Lincoln Chapel Cemetery, Laurelton, Union Co, PA
dau. of Royal Cressinger and Gertrude Slagenwhite Cressinger
mar. Robert Bilger, June 4, 1934

She came to Weikert in 1934. Sunday school teacher at Hironimus Church in 1950–7. They lived in the Levan property next to the store, then in Reid Pursley's home that burned down, then Jim Bilger's place of 145 acres; and once in the Aimetti farm house. In the 60s or 70s they built the Paskovich house. She worked with Bob at their saw mill for seven years at the bridge up from Paskovich's. She bought property from Leroy R. Goodlander between 1989 and 1993.

Children: David, Gertrude Bertha (*b.* Aug. 30, 1936), Benjamin James (*b.* March 28, 1938), Roberta Pauline (*b.* April 13, 1941).

Miriam A. Montague
    Mrs. William Wilson
b. Aug. 6, 1905, Muncy, Lycoming Co, PA
d. June 24, 1962, Coal Twsp, Northumberland Co, PA
bur. Watsontown Cemetery, Northumberland Co, PA
dau. of William Montague and Carrie M. Johe Montague
mar. William Wilson

As widow, Al Goodlander's housekeeper. Lived 30 years in Weikert. She had been a messenger and mail carrier. In 1940 census she was listed as a winder in a silk mill.

[F.A.G. 143635925]

(permission: Jerry Sholter)

REBA C. "REBIE" KOONSMAN
MRS. CHARLES E. WENRICH
b. Oct. 6, 1900
d. Nov. 19, 1945
bur. St. Peter's (Ray's) Church Cemetery, Hartleton, Union Co, PA
dau. of William W. Koonsman and Cora C. Koonsman
mar. Charles E. Wenrich, July 31, 1919, White Springs UMC Church, Union Co

Lived at Lindale. She was a member of Hironimus Union Church. In 1903 she was in the Children's Day Program of Hironimus Union Church. In 1909 she was in the Girls' Primary Sunday School class at Hironimus Union Church. In 1910 census she was 9 years old. She was named in White Springs UMC Circuit history. She taught Sunday school at Hironimus Union Church.

Children: Cora Lillian Wenrich (*mar.* Henry Gast "Smokey" Stover).

[F.A.G. 125546971]

HAZEL MUNSON?
MRS. EVALD G. EDBERG
mar. Evald G. Edberg

Supposedly Mrs. Edberg came to Weikert when her husband was with the CCC Camp. They lived in the George Libby house on the corner of Weikert Road and Weikert Lane (now White Mountain Road). They supposedly came from Johnstown (probably Jamestown), New York. Mrs.

Edberg lent books to the neighbors. She had Weikert women in to quilt and was a beautiful sewer. They may have lived in Weikert for three years. She was Assistant Sunday School Supervisor at Hironimus Union Church in 1934.

Children: Janet, married George Sholter Sr.; their daughter was Beverly Sholter.

(permission: Tim Bastian)

IRENE ELIZABETH STAUDINGER
 MRS. EDWARD C. GALER
b. July 24, 1908
d. Dec. 13, 1967
bur. Hironimus Union Church Cemetery, Weikert, Union Co, PA
mar. Edward C. Galer

Lived on west side of White Mountain Road, Weikert. In 1930 census they were living with Zach Galer, 83, and his housekeeper, Phoebe S., 61. She was on Hironimus Union Church Memory List in 1967. She was known to love navy beans.

Children: foster-son Clarence Carpenter (*b.* 1926, Pardee, *d.* 1995), adoptive (?) daughter Kathy.

[F.A.G. 91825494]

Irene E.
Galer
(permission:
Bill Cunningham)

PAULINE ANN CREBS
    MRS. WILLIAM E. LEVAN
b. Jan. 8, 1929, Sunbury, Northumberland Co, PA
d. June 22, 2015, Millmont, Union Co, PA
bur. Northumberland Memorial Park, Stonington, Northumberland Co, PA
dau. of Paul S. Crebs and Florence V. Rowe Crebs
mar. William E. LeVan Jr.

    Lived at 5570 Weikert Road, Weikert. Her family first came to Weikert in 1937 with their friends the Fishers of Mitchell Lane. She was first in her high school class and class secretary. She was a member and worthy matron of Eastern Star and White Shrine and a cub scout den mother. Early on she was the secretary for her father's moving business. She had property along the creek near the bridge. Her good friends were Marge Bilger, Verna Sholter, Cora Barnett Lamey Boop, Katie Minium Ely.
    Children: Jody P., William C.

(permission:
William E.
Levan Jr.)

OLIVE R. MILLER
MRS. GEORGE R. LIBBY
b. 1888 or 1889
d. 1983
bur. Northampton Memorial Shrine, Easton, Northampton Co, PA
mar. George R. Libby

She was from Millerstown, Perry Co, PA. In 1930 census House 5, she was 41, he was 40.

Children (in 1930 census): Beatrice, 16, Ruth L., 14, C. Clinton, 12, Helen M., 9, George R. Jr., 8, W. Miller, 6.
[F.A.G. 168622452]

(permission: Wirt/Boop)

(MARIAN) ROSELLA CANOUSE or KNAUSS
MRS. JOHN RUSSELL LIBBY
b. Oct. 21, 1905, Lewis Twsp, Union Co, PA
d. May 21, 1957, Williamsport, Lycoming Co, PA
bur. Hartleton Cemetery, Union Co, PA
dau. of Jacob Edward and Anna M. Aikey Knauss
mar. John Russell Libby

Children: Harry Wade (*b.* Jan. 18, 1926)

MARY (PECK)
MRS. CHARLES PECK
b. around 1898
mar. Charles Peck

In 1930 census House 2, he was 48, she was 32; boarder William Bettilyon, 32.

Children (in 1930 census): Edna, 15, Samuel L., 11, Charles Jr., 9, William O., 3.

ELIZABETH "BETTY" LORRAINE KISSINGER
  MRS. HERMAN FREDERICK REICH
  MRS. HARRY L. SNOOK
b. Feb. 23, 1915, Sunbury, Northumberland Co, PA
d. July 2, 2003, Hartley Twsp, Union Co, PA
bur. Hironimus Union Church Cemetery, Weikert, Union Co, PA
dau. of Allen K. and Mabel Keefer Kissinger
mar. 1. Herman Frederick Reich, 1933
mar. 2. Harry L. Snook

Lived at "Avian Haven," 8035 Weikert Road, Weikert, PA. She inherited this property through her marriage to Herman Reich, son of Kate Reich Korten. She was a member of Ebeneezer United Church of Christ Laurelton and the Laurelton Women's Club. She was tax collector for Hartley Township. In the late 1960s or early '70s, Betty donated her father Allen Kissinger's baby grand piano to Hironimus Union Church.
  [F.A.G. 91828596]

(permission: Lee Kissinger)

BARBARA "BOBBIE" RUTH BARNET
  MRS. HAROLD CRONIN
b. July 22, 1934, Weikert, Union Co, PA
d. March 24, 2016, Hartleton, Union Co, PA
bur. Hironimus Union Church Cemetery, Weikert, Union Co, PA
dau. of Jonas William Barnet and Virginia Gertrude Libby Barnet Bettilyon
mar. Harold R. Cronin, May 18, 1953

She was a U.S. Air Force veteran. She co-owned the Weikert Store for seven years. She worked at the Muncy State Correctional Institution. She was a member of the Hironimus Union Church and taught Sunday school in 1947. In 1951 she donated an altar painting of Christ in Gethsemane by Mrs. Charles Dorman (Kay Lomison) to the Hironimus Union Church in memory of her father, Jonas William Barnet, and great-great-uncle, Jonas John Barnett.

Children: Chivi Marie (*mar.* Dagg), Lyman Ray, Patrick Erin, Michelle Ann.

[F.A.G. 161495613]

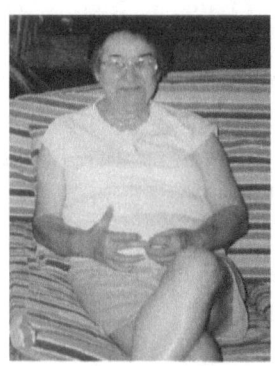

(permission: August Barnett and Geri Willen)

AMELIA JANE "MICKEY" KALER
MRS. ROBERT KERMIT ELY
b. Oct. 24, 1916, Millmont, Lewis Twsp, Union Co, PA
d. Feb. 12, 2004, Lewisburg, Union Co, PA
bur. Hartleton Cemetery, Union Co, PA
dau. of Milton E. Kahler and Mamie Willowfern Blyler Kahler
mar. Robert Kermit Ely, Sept. 10, 1940

They lived at 5205 Weikert Rd., Weikert, PA. She operated "Mickey's Lunch" next to their home in the late 1940s and early 1950s. She retired from the Laurelton Center after more than twenty years of service. In 1951 she taught Sunday school at Hironimus Union Church.

Children: Jimmy Robert (*b.* 1942), Jane Amelia (*mar.* Paul Foster, April 29, 1978, and had Paul Michael Foster).

[F.A.G. 10410262]

circa 1952
(permission:
Jane Ely Foster)

VELMA NADINE (OR NADENE) LAYTON
   MRS. BENJAMIN THOMAS GOODLANDER
b. Aug. 17, 1910, Warfordsburg, Fulton Co, PA
d. March 24, 1979, Lewisburg, Union Co, PA
bur. Lincoln Chapel Cemetery, Laurelton, Union Co, PA
dau. of Alfred Simon Layton and Lillie May Wink Layton
mar. Benjamin Thomas Goodlander (after his divorce in 1938)

She lived in Weikert, on the east side of White Mountain Road near the bridge, from 1945 until her death. Hironimus Church Memory List of 1979. Letters Testamentary 1900–1999, Union County Courthouse.

[F.A.G. 75075451]

(permission:
Jane Ely Foster)

MARY LOU KLINE
   MRS. JERE L. ENGLE
b. May 30, 1925, Shamokin, Northumberland Co, PA
d. May 20, 2005
dau. of Harry L. Kline and Helen M. Hoy Kline
mar. Jere L. Engle, July 25, 1948, Shamokin

They lived at 832 Jolly's Grove Lane, Weikert, PA. She came originally as a baby to her grandparents at the Hoys' cabin. 1943 graduate of Shamokin High. A graduate of East Stroudsburg State Teachers' College, she was a school teacher for thirty years before retiring to Weikert. She was a substitute pianist at Hironimus Church. Lifelong member of First Presbyterian Church, Shamokin. She was known for her tollhouse cookies and enjoyed knitting and needlework.

Children: Jere L., Jay A., Jeff B.

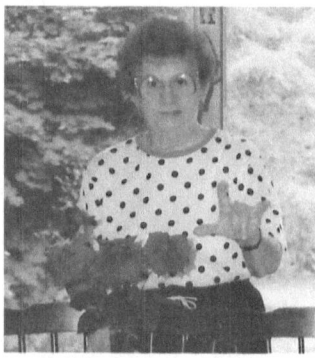

(permission: Jere L. Engle)

VIOLET MAY PEARSON
    MRS. JAMES GLAUS
b. Oct. 25, 1919, Ridgeway, PA
d. July 12, 2005, Easton, Northampton Co, PA
cremated
dau. of George Pearson and Zepha Pearson
mar. James Glaus

Vi served in the U.S. Navy. She raised her "boys" at a Little Mountain campsite, then a cabin "Glaus Haus," Little Mountain Lane, Weikert. A recreational resident who spent much of the year at Weikert, she was related to several other West End families and was considered a true friend and wonderful neighbor.

Children: Scott, William, Jeff.

(permission: Scott Glaus)

GLADYS GERALDINE BINGAMAN
MRS. FLOYD WASHINGTON HARVEY
b. Dec. 8, 1911, Hartley Twsp, Union Co, PA
d. Sept. 6, 2004, Millmont, Union Co, PA
bur. Hironimus Union Church Cemetery, Weikert, Union Co, PA
dau. of Simon Showalter Bingaman and Cora Louise Sholter Bingaman
mar. Floyd Washington Harvey, Dec. 1, 1933, Forty Fort, Luzerne Co, PA

Lived at 5440 Weikert Road, Weikert, in 1940 census House 21. She had been a cook at Wesley Forest Camp for many years and was said to be a wonderful bread baker.

Children: Kathryn E., Betty L., Richard James (*b.* Sept. 30, 1939), Floyd Earl (*b.* Nov. 9, 1942), Daniel Robert (*b.* Sept. 10, 1944), Terry Lee (*b.* Sept. 17, 1947), David Wayne (*b.* June 16, 1949), Galen William (*b.* Dec. 11, 1950). Richard, Floyd, Daniel, Terry and David were *bap.* White Springs UMC Circuit on April 9, 1950, Galen on March 25, 1951.

[F.A.G. 99956116]

(permission: Danny Harvey)

Virginia Kathryn "Jean" Ely
Mrs. Max Schneeberg

b. March 1912, Hartleton, Union Co, PA
d. Jan. 6, 1991, Williamsport, Lycoming Co, PA
bur. Hironimus Union Church Cemetery, Weikert, Union Co, PA
dau. of William Henry Ely and Alice Elizabeth Snyder Ely
mar. Max Schneeberg, *div.* July 1956

She spent much of her childhood with Uncle William "Billy" Valentine and Carrie Snyder Valentine. She served with the Women's Army Nurse Corps as a Captain. Graduated from Jefferson Medical College School of Nursing, graduated from Bucknell University with a B.A. degree and subsequently an M.A. in Economics In 1954 she was Director of Nursing at Laurelton State School and Hospital.

Children: David

[F.A.G. 97333182]

(permission: Jane Ely Foster)

Sara "Sally" L. Galer
Mrs. George J. Sholter

b. July 7, 1918, Vintondale, Cambria Co, PA
d. Jan. 23, 1997, Lewisburg, Union Co, PA
bur. Hironimus Union Church Cemetery, Weikert, Union Co, PA
dau. of John Galer and Elizabeth Jenkins Galer
mar. George J. Sholter Sr., July 19, 1941, Weikert

She graduated from Nanty-Glo High School in 1937. In 1947–51 and 1980 she taught Sunday school at Hironimus Union Church. In 1970–94 she was Weikert postmaster, having worked previously at the Laurelton

Center business office as secretary. Member of Laurelton Women's Club, Order of the Eastern Star.

Children: George J. "Jerry" (*b.* Dec. 28, 1943), Sandra Lee (*b.* March 10, 1942, *mar.* Mills), Gail F. (*mar.* Ulrich). George and Sandra were *bap.* April 21, 1946, White Springs UMC Circuit, together with their mother.

[F.A.G. 99956162]

(permission: Tim Bastian, Jerry Sholter)

AGNES JEAN WALLACE
    MRS. CLEMUEL STIMELING
b. June 1892, 1882, or 1889
d. Sept. 27, 1959
bur. Hartleton Cemetery, Hartleton, Union Co, PA
dau. of Joseph L. Wallace and Hannah M. Sholter
mar. Clemuel Stimeling

Clemuel was a son of William Stimeling and Mary Alice Sholter. He was *b.* June 11, 1882, at Cherry Run and *d.* Sept. 3, 1968, in Lewisburg. His letters testamentary of 1968 and 1971, Union County Courthouse. Lesta Stimeling may be his second wife.

Children: Florence Alberta Stimeling (*d.* Sept. 24, 1959?).
[F.A.G. 10411393]

HATTIE BLANCHE JOLLY
    MRS. THOMAS W. SHOLTER
    MRS. ROBERT C. THARP
b. Oct. 9, 1879, in PA
d. Jan. 22, 1967
bur. Hartleton Hill Cemetery, Hartleton, Union Co, PA
dau. of Allen Seymour Jolley and Nancy Jane Zimmerman Jolley

mar. 1. Thomas W. Sholter, May 28, 1899, Weikert, PA
mar. 2. Robert C. Tharp, Oct. 6, 1923

Resident of Pardee, but with Weikert P.O. Box in the 1940s. Co-owner of Tharp's Tavern and store, Pardee. In 1947–51 she was a Sunday school teacher at Hironimus Union Church. In 1967 she was on the Hironimus Union Church Memory Roll. 1967 Letters Testamentary, Union County Courthouse.

[F.A.G. 1041147]

GENEVIEVE "GIGI" FRIGGLE
  MRS. EARL P. WEASER
b. Feb. 3, 1903, Franklin, Venango Co, PA
d. March 31, 1994, Lewisburg, Union Co, PA
bur. Franklin Cemetery, Franklin, Venango Co, PA
dau. of William Friggle and Mattie Maude Friggle
mar. Earl P. Weaser (*d.* 1961)

Lived on Weikert Road, Weikert. In 1943 they bought 24 acres. She was a member of Laurelton Women's Club, Ebenezer Church of Christ in Laurelton, Hironimus Union Church, Union County Sportsmen's Club (also stockholder), and American Legion Post No. 44 (life member). In her younger days Genevieve rode a mule on a rural circuit through Tennessee, taking materials for craft projects to the women in Appalachia and then returning to pick up the finished items to sell for the women to earn a little extra income. She was later a buyer for women's items for the J. C. Penney department store. She was an accomplished quilter.

circa 1923
(permission:
Bill Cunningham)

Women of Weikert

ETHEL RIPPEL
   MRS. RAYMOND BURROWES WINTER
b. Aug. 17, 1905, McKeesport, Allegheny Co, PA
d. July 1974
bur. Webster Cemetery, Huntersville, Lycoming Co, PA
dau. of John F. Rippel and Priscilla Rowland Rippel
mar. Raymond Burrowes "Foxy" Winter, Aug. 14, 1941

Raymond (*b.* 1881, *d.* 1968) purchased land for their home at "Aumiller Bottom" from along Penns Creek further west than Cherry Run, at the far west end of Winter Road. Ethel taught at the Hartley Township High School, Laurelton, Union Co. In 1983 she sold 415 acres with 3.8 stream miles to the Pennsylvania Fish Commission for $15,547.

[F.A.G. 143225748]

BETTY LOUISE SHOWERS
   MRS. WERREN LEE WINTERSTEEN
b. March 30, 1928
d. April 11, 1994
bur. Ward Memorial Cemetery, Brookings, Curry Co, Oregon
mar. Werren Wintersteen

They lived at what is now 303 MAG Way off Aimetti Lane. Moved back to the West around 1978.

Children: Ginger (*mar.* Egnew), Lee, Sherry (*mar.* Magnuson), Gary, Linda (*mar.* Halley), Robin, Timothy, Mary (*mar.* Welch), David, Alan.

[F.A.G. 46828646]

MARTHA JEAN KRICK
   MRS. ADAM MARTIN YOCUM
b. June 25, 1916, Harrisburg, Dauphin Co, PA
d. Oct. 6, 2004, Milton, Northumberland Co, PA
bur. Harmony Cemetery, Milton, Northumberland Co, PA
dau. of Maurice Hanson Krick and Grace V. Lamine Krick
mar. Adam Martin Yocum, July 26, 1939

In her early life she taught school in Weikert, eight grades, and lived with Kathryn and Jake Barnet. She was a member of St. Andrew's UMC in Milton, PA.

Children: Carole J. (*mar.* Bower), Nancy L. (*mar.* Shearer), Hilda Kay

(*mar.* Morgan), Adam M.
[F.A.G. 102524179]

(permission:
Nancy Shearer)

Jane Elizabeth Beaver
   Mrs. Donald L. Kline
b. June 27, 1917, in PA
d. Oct. 6, 1997, in PA
bur. St. Peter's Reformed Cemetery, Paxinos, Northumberland Co, PA
dau. of J. Raymond Beaver and Hazel G. McMinn Rittenburg Beaver
mar. Donald L. Kline

She worked at Laurelton State Village. She was an independent woman who loved Weikert, fishing, and the mountains. She and Donald met at a camp on Penns Creek. She was from Mifflinburg. Their families spent all summers at their cabins in Jolly's Grove Lane, Weikert.

Children: Donna (*mar.* Jim Slaughter), Donald S. Jr., Patty (*mar.* Severn).
[F.A.G. 145563388]

(permission:
Donna K.
Slaughter)

Women of Weikert

ALICE ETHEL CODLING
b. Nov. 2, 1896, Deptford, London, England
d. Aug. 8, 1953, Mifflinburg, Union Co, PA
bur. West Side Cemetery (Orchard Hill Cemetery), Shamokin Dam, Snyder Co, PA
dau. of Elijah John Codling (blacksmith) and Elizabeth Emma Stevens Codling

She had a cabin on Mitchell Lane, second or third structure below the Weikert Bridge. She inherited her property from her Uncle Henry Lynn and she was a recreational resident. She lived in Sunbury with the Reichenbach family on S. 4th Street. She died while shopping in Mifflinburg with Amelia "Mickey" Ely and Jane Ely Foster.

[F.A.G. 170405608]

(permission: Jane Ely Foster)

PANSY A. CALLAHAN
    MRS. RICHARD W. JORDAN
b. May 12, 1930, Dunbar, Fayette Co, PA
d. Sept. 13, 2016, Hartleton, Union Co, PA
bur. Hillview Cemetery, Greensburg, Westmoreland Co, PA
dau. of Thomas Callahan and Pansy Hughes Callahan
mar. Richard "Dick" W. Jordan

Her husband sometimes called her "Cookie" or shortened to "Cook." In later life she resided with Toni and Dallas Klauger.

Children: Toni (*mar.* Dallas Klauger), Diane (*mar.* Wagner), Tracy (*mar.* Buswell), Scott R.

[F.A.G. 169903536]

(permission: Toni Klauger)

JEAN HOWELL ADAMS
    MRS. JOSEPH ROLAND SHOLTER
    MRS. MYRON LEON ERDLEY
b. Sept. 9, 1929, Union Co, PA
d. Feb. 22, 2014, Hope Mills, North Carolina
bur. Hironimus Union Church Cemetery, Weikert, Union Co, PA
dau. of Floyd Adams and Alberta/Albreta Howell Adams
mar. 1. Joseph Roland Sholter, 1948, *div.* April 1970
mar. 2. Myron Leon Erdley

Lived on Weikert Road, Weikert, PA. She taught Sunday school in 1957 at Hironimus Union Church, and in 1968 she was one of the last three Sunday School teachers when the Hironimus Sunday School closed. She was Weikert Postmaster in 1968–70 and helped run the Weikert Store.

Children: Joseph Lawrence (*b.* Feb. 6, 1949, in Lewisburg, drowned in 1954 and *bur.* Hironimus Cemetery), Patti Lee (*mar.* Melvin Drumheller), David Roland (*mar.* Heidelinde Havice), Laurie Jean (*mar.* George Bloom Jr.)

(permission: Jerry Sholter, Tim Bastian)

Thelma Leona Lamey
   Mrs. L. Roy Himmelreich
b. July 6, 1920
d. April 1984
mar. L. Roy Himmelreich, 1941

They lived at Cherry Run. Fire leveled their home in Oct. 1960. Last known place of residence was Hollidaysburg, Blair Co, PA.

Children: L. Roy Jr., Carol (*b.* 1964, *d.* 1982), Anna Linn Knight Gibbs (*b.* 1948, *d.* Aug. 8, 2008, Jacksonville, Florida), Dale or Leland McKenney, Mary (*mar.* Colyer), Nathan, April (*mar.* Yost), Jackie.

Virginia Mae "Ginny" Engleman
   Mrs. Franklin B. Steese
b. March 27, 1920, New Berlin, Union Co, PA
d. July 7, 1982, Danville, Montour Co, PA
bur. Hartleton Cemetery, Hartleton, Union Co, PA
dau. of John Engleman and Myrtle Solomon Engleman
mar. Franklin B. Steese, 1938

Ginny was a Steward at the Union County Sportsmen's Club in the 1950s and '60s and was employed there later during a difficult time for the Club. There is a flagpole at the front of the Club dedicated to her memory. She was a fixture in the social life of residents and recreational campers in the "West End."

(permission: Judy Blair)

Joan Maxine Auten
b. Nov. 1, 1935, Sunbury, Northumberland Co, PA
d. March 15, 2006, Weikert, Union Co, PA
bur. Pomfret Manor Cemetery, Northumberland Co, PA
dau. of John M. Auten and Blanche E. Zettlemoyer Auten

Joan owned O-Ten Ranch, 6885 Weikert Road, Weikert. She had been coming to the area for many years as her parents owned and ran a camp downstream. She bought her property in 1961 and resided there until her death in 2006. She was a member of the Order of the Eastern Star. In 1996 she was a Sunday School teacher at Hironimus Union Church and a vice-President of the Congregation. In 1997 she was a member of the West End Library Board of Trustees and in 2001 Vice President of the Board. In the 1987–8 era she was President of the Union County Sportsmen's Club and dressed as and played Santa Claus. She was a graduate of West Chester State Teacher's College with a B.S. Degree in Health and Physical Education. Her M.Ed. Degree was from East Stroudsburg University. She retired as Associate Professor Emeritus of Health and Physical Education at Bloomsburg State University after a tenure of 19 years. At Bloomsburg she directed the Women's Co-educational Intramural Sports Program.

There is a $1000 Joan M. Auten Memorial Kinesiology Scholarship at West Chester University for students, particularly women from Lackawanna, Luzerne and Wyoming Counties of PA.

(permission: John Auten)

BARBARA LOUISE "CHUBBY" PAVELIC
   MRS. MICHAEL S. GASTON
   MRS. EDWARD T. BARNET
b. June 1, 1918, Harrisburg, Dauphin Co, PA
d. Jan. 2, 2006, Carlisle, Cumberland Co, PA
bur. Hironimus Union Church Cemetery, Weikert, Union Co, PA
dau. of John Pavelic and Anna Pavelic
mar. 1. Michael S. Gaston, Oct. 1, 1937
mar. 2. Edward T. Barnet, Jan. 1969

She was employed at New Cumberland Army Depot.
Children: Maryann (*mar.* Losik) and Martin Gaston.
[F.A.G. 91828239]

circa 2002
(permission:
Mary Ann Losik)

MRS. WARREN BECK
dau. of Florence Alberta Miller
mar. Warren Beck

Granddaughter of Clem Stimeling (*bur.* Hartleton Cemetery), with whom she was living when he died in Weikert in 1968.

NATALIE JOANN "JO" HARNE
  MRS. WILLIAM DAVID ELY
b. July 17, 1927, Waynesboro, Franklin Co, PA
d. Dec. 5, 2002, Weikert, Union Co, PA
Cremated, ashes scattered.
dau. of Norris Allen Harne and Hazel Miller Harne
mar. William David "Bill" Ely, Dec. 19, 1945

Around 1960 they built on Weikert Road, Weikert. She was an attendant at the Laurelton State School. She and Bill owned and operated Ickey's Bar and Grill in Milton. She enjoyed hunting and fishing.

Children: William Allen, Robert M.
[F.A.G. 130065153]

circa 1982
(permission:
Jane Ely Foster)

NELLIE M. PICK
    MRS. CHARLES G. RHEPPARD
b. March 15, 1892
d. Dec. 1969
bur. Hironimus Union Church Cemetery, Weikert, Union Co, PA
dau. of Levi Pick and Kate Bartley Pick
mar. Charles G. Rheppard

    In 1969 she was remembered on Hironimus Union Church Memory List.

    [F.A.G. 99956146]

Nellie M.
Rheppard
(permission:
Bill Cunningham)

JENNIE MARGARET ZIMMERMAN
    MRS. WILMER HERBERT SCHWENK
b. Feb. 26, 1910, Pine Grove Twsp, Schuylkill Co, PA
d. Jan. 21, 2005, Lewisburg, Union Co, PA
bur. St. Peter's Church Cemetery, Pine Grove, PA
dau. of David Zimmerman and Margaret Zimmerman
mar. Wilmer Herbert Schwenk, Sept. 2, 1933, Orwigsburg, PA

Graduated from Pine Grove High School in 1928. She attended Harrisburg Beauty School and was a self-employed beautician for twenty years. Life long member of St. Peter's Evangelical Lutheran Church, Pine Grove. He was from Cressona, Schuylkill Co, PA. They owned a cabin at 178 Jolly's Grove Lane as early as 1960.

Children: Carl N., Shirley L. (*mar.* Weand), David, Bruce.

CATHERINE W. (SPECK)
MRS. FRANK E. SPECK?
b. 1898
d. 1963
bur. Hironimus Union Church Cemetery, Weikert, Union Co, PA
mar. Frank. E Speck?

In 1963 on Hironimus Union Church Memory List.
[F.A.G. 91826502]

Catherine W. Speck
(permission: Bill Cunningham)

KATHRYN MARY WEINHOFFER
MRS. MICHAEL CARL ZYRY
b. Oct. 25, 1921, Coal Twsp, Northumberland Co, PA
d. March 13, 2001, Watsontown, Northumberland Co, PA
bur. All Saints Cemetery, Elysburg, Northumberland Co, PA
dau. of Frank Weinhoffer and Mary C. Feibig Weinhoffer
mar. Michael Carl Zyry, Aug. 1938, Hagerstown, Maryland

It is believed that they moved to Weikert in 1964; lived on what is now MAG Way. She was a machine operator in the garment industry for her entire career. Known for her hospitality, she was a homebody who canned and gardened and made her own wine. She was known for her soups and enjoyed handicrafts. Eventually she moved to Mifflinburg member of St. George Church.

Children: Paul Raymond (*d.* 2010), Robert Francis (*d.* 2012), Michael Roman "Mick" (*d.* 2014), Ruby Louise, Barbara Ann.
[F.A.G. 153098067]

MARGARET RUTH KURTZ
    MRS. PAUL EUGENE KANOUR
b. July 12, 1907, Port Royal, Juniata Co, PA
d. Sept. 8, 1997, Lewisburg, Union Co, PA
bur. Lincoln Chapel Cemetery, Laurelton, Union Co, PA
dau. of Samuel Ira Kurtz and Olive Neiman Haines Kurtz
mar. Paul E. Kanour, April 25, 1930

Resided in Weikert from 1970. She was employed by Bell Telephone Company as a telephone operator. Member of Laurelton Women's Club and Christ's United Lutheran Church, Millmont.

Children: Nancy Ruth (*mar.* Spearing), Eugene K.
[F.A.G. 100507443]

RHODA JEANETTE HILE
    MRS. ROBERT OMER CURTIS KLINE
b. Dec. 5, 1910, Sunbury, Northumberland Co, PA
d. April 25, 1997, Hartleton, Union Co, PA
bur. Hironimus Union Church Cemetery, Weikert, Union Co, PA
dau. of Clement Hile and Bessie A. Gouchnour Hile
mar. Robert Omer Curtis Kline, 1927

She was a veteran of the Women's Army Corps and was discharged from active service on Aug. 20, 1993, at Cochran Field, Georgia. She was considered a veteran for burial. She retired from General Electric in Philadelphia as a lab assistant.

Children: Ronald.
[F.A.G. 5579803]

Rhoda J. Kline
(permission:
Bill Cunningham)

Women of Weikert

ARMENA ELIZABETH BURKMAN
    MRS. ROBERT LEROY NEUHAUSER
b. Feb. 25, 1895 or 1893, Compassville, Chester Co, PA.
d. Feb. 23, 1990
bur. Bellevue Presbyterian Cemetery, Gap, Lancaster Co, PA
dau. of Conrad R. Burkman and Adeline Plank Burkman
mar. Robert Leroy Neuhauser

She had a small stone cabin in downtown Weikert probably built by Bob Bilger before moving to a trailer across the road from Vi and George Neuhauser. She was a cook for AFWREO ("All Fellows Will Respect Each Other") hunting camp. She was a full time resident of Weikert from 1978. Robert's death certificate has Armena's last name as Sando.
    [F.A.G. 77587930]

(permission: Seth Neuhauser)

MARY S. NEUHAUSER
b. 1900
d. 1975
bur. Bellevue Presbyterian Cemetery, Gap, Lancaster Co, PA
dau. of Joseph Neuhauser and Elizabeth Stoltzfus Neuhauser

She lived in the big house ("Pine Acres," now "Walnut Hill Farm") next to the Weikert store with her sisters Sadie C. Neuhauser and Helen W. Ammon. They sold to the Levans around 1973 and moved to Bethlehem, PA.
    [F.A.G. 77504326]

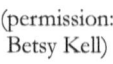
(permission: Betsy Kell)

RUTH M. KOBEL
  MRS. ELERY E. NEWBERRY
b. in PA
mar. Elery E. Newberry (*b.* 1905, *d.* 1988)

Lived on Jolly's Grove Lane permanently after Elery retired from teaching school in Shamokin. According to the tax list the building was built in 1948 and sold to Marlin and Joyce Kerstetter in 1995. Ruth was said to be part Native American.

Children: Kathryn E. (*b.* 1927, *d.* 1931 of scarlet fever).

DORIS (REED)
  MRS. DAVID REED

She lived at Lindale in the home that burned. It had been Roy Ott's beer garden, "Mountain Inn," now the Kerry Wenrick property. They were there for a period of time between 1970 and 1987. He was supervisor of a Lewisburg nursing home. She worked in real estate.

ANNE (MARYANNE) WOJESKI
  MRS. CLIFFORD CLARK SCHOENING
b. Feb. 2, 1912, Newark, New Jersey
d. April 26, 2009, Rolling Hills Manor, Millmont
bur. Hironimus Union Church Cemetery, Weikert, Union Co, PA
dau. of Michael Wojeski and Tilka Fidunak Wojeski
mar. Clifford Clark Schoening (*d.* 1960)

Moved to the Jolly farm house in Jolly's Grove Lane, Weikert, in 1975. She loved the Weikert quiet and peace of mind. She enjoyed gardening, crocheting, and daily reading of her Bible. She cooked for herself and loved venison. Her grandson fished from her property and her granddaughters had tea with her daily. She and her two sisters worked in rocket assembly in Roselle, New Jersey, during W.W.II.

Children: Phyllis S. (*mar.* Latherow, of Madera, PA), Barbara L. (*mar.* Frank Paskovich, of Weikert).

[F.A.G. 91827906]

(permission: Barbara Paskovich)

LOUISE "WEEZIE" GOEHRING
MRS. JAMES C. SCOTT
b. Jan. 31, 1937, Pittsburgh, PA
d. Nov. 27, 1997, Durham, Connecticut
dau. of Raymond Goehring and Louise Glover Goehring
mar. James C. Scott, 1961

A recreational resident of Little Mountain and Westfall at Trail's End. She was a graduate of Mt. Holyoke College, and received a Ph.D. in Art History from the University of Wisconsin. A Union County local historian, she studied family life, work and women's lives around the turn of the twentieth century in western Union County. She was working on a book-length manuscript on the social history of "Cabins in the Woods," with special emphasis on the "West End" of Union County.

Children: Mia L., Aaron P., Noah R.

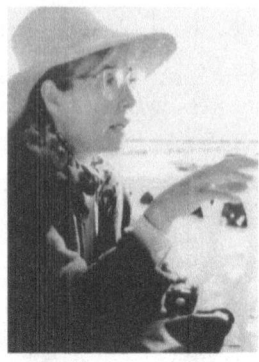

(permission: James Scott, David Goehring)

ALDA MAY "BLONDIE" READER
  MRS. AMMON J. C. SHAFFER
b. May 4, 1929, Rockefeller Twsp, Northumberland Co, PA
d. July 4, 2001, Danville, Montour Co, PA
bur. Hironimus Union Church Cemetery, Weikert, Union Co, PA
dau. of Herbert Felker Reader and Maude Louise Campbell Reader
mar. Ammon J. C. Shaffer, July 21, 1961, Hagerstown, Maryland

A thirty-year resident, she lived on Weikert Road at Little Mountain. She retired as a nurse's aide. In 1996 she sold her property to Don Eckrod Jr. for $60,000. The property had passed through four generations of Shaffer men and women since 1818.

Children: Janet Marie (*d.* 1961), Christine Beth (*mar.* Mann), Donna Darlene.

P. JOAN HANSELMAN
  MRS. ORVILLE L. SPANGLER
b. May 27, 1940, Rochester, New York
d. March 1, 2007, Lewisburg, Union Co, PA
bur. New Berlin Cemetery, Union Co, PA
dau. of Carl E. Hanselman and Lola Gwen Ranck Hanselman
mar. Orville L. "Bear" Spangler, Feb. 9, 1974, Marysville, PA

Recreational resident, lived at 966 Aimetti Lane. She began coming to Weikert in 1970. In 1989–91 she was President of the Union County Sportsmen's Club. There is a flagpole in her memory in front of the Club. She was a turkey hunter and interested in travel. She was a member of the Messiah Lutheran Church, New Berlin. Manager of Selinsgrove Senior

Center for thirty years; member of Selinsgrove Order of the Eastern Star.
Children: Steve Eaton, Jill (*mar.* Schambach), Lisa (*mar.* Showers).

(permission: Orville Spangler)

MILDRED FLORENCE HIRONIMUS
MRS. CHARLES WILLIAM TEICHMAN
b. June 28, 1909, Oldtown, Allegany Co, Maryland
d. Nov. 23, 1999, Lewisburg, Union Co, PA
bur. Hartleton Cemetery, Hartleton, Union Co, PA
dau. of James McCellan Hironimus and Margaret Adele Galer Hironimus
mar. Charles William Teichman, Nov. 23, 1927, Millmont, PA

She was a matron in Johnson Cottage, Laurelton State School. In 1980 she was one of five members of a newly formed non-profit corporation for Hironimus Union Church. She was a member of Laurelton Women's Club, the Union County Historical Society, the Pennsylvania Association of Retired State Employees, and Ebenezer United Church of Christ, Laurelton. 1999 Letters Testamentary, Union County Court House.

Children: Mary Elaine (*b.* around 1928, *d.* 2008, *mar. 1.* Dohrmann, *mar. 2.* Genevish), Seibert "Herb" (*mar.* Connie Snook).

(permission: Herb. Teichman)

Minerva Gertrude Klauger
Mrs. Clarence Frederick Umlauf
b. Feb. 5, 1905, Lavelle, Schuylkill Co, PA
d. March 4, 2003, Lewisburg, Union Co, PA
bur. Citizens Cemetery, Schuylkill Co, PA
dau. of William L. Klauger and Mollie C. Slotterback Klauger
mar. Clarence Frederick Umlauf, Nov. 24, 1927

Lived at 6515 Weikert Road, Weikert, PA. She moved to Weikert when she was aged to live with her brother Harold and his wife Alma Klauger. She and Clarence are buried next to her parents.

[F.A.G. 128127003]

(permission: Toni Klauger)

Catherine Delores Cooney
Mrs. Lewis W. Klauger
b. July 17, 1918, Philadelphia, PA
d. Jan. 27, 2009, Weikert, Union Co, PA
bur. Citizens Cemetery, Lavelle, Schuylkill Co, PA
dau. of Richard Cooney and Catherine Cardin Cooney
mar. Lewis W. Klauger, 1934

Lived at 91 Buick Boulevard, Weikert. Moved to Weikert in 1995, but had been coming for years. She was a seamstress, manufacturing flags and camouflage uniforms in World War II; she was also a quilter.

Children: Charles W., Lewis W.

[F.A.G. 33335986]

(permission:
Charles Klauger)

VIOLET REGINA PROSSER
   MRS. GEORGE R. NEUHAUSER
b. March 26, 1916, Coatesville, Chester Co, PA
d. Feb. 17, 2005
bur. Hironimus Union Church Cemetery, Weikert, Union Co, PA
dau. of William Henry Prosser and Annie Clyde Prosser
mar. George Roy Neuhauser, Oct, 21, 1941, Winthrop, Massachusetts

   Vi and George lived in several cities while he was an airline pilot. They retired to 7715 Weikert Road, Weikert. She was a graduate of Chester County Area High School. She enjoyed knitting, crocheting, making hooked rugs, and playing her home organ. She was almost blind later in life.

   Children: Seth G.
[F.A.G. 99956134]

(permission:
Seth Neuhauser)

ELIZABETH JANE MARTIN
    MRS. KERRY L. WENRICK
b. March 31, 1972, Allentown, Lehigh Co, PA
d. April 5, 2006, Haines Twsp, Centre Co, PA
bur. Hironimus Union Church Cemetery, Weikert, Union Co, PA
dau. of John F. Martin and Victoria Vandergrift Martin
mar. Kerry L. Wenrick, May 17, 1997, Lewisburg, PA

They lived at 6545 Weikert Road, Weikert. She grew up at PA Forestry Headquarters on Route 45 and was a resident of Weikert for 11 years. She was a 1990 graduate of Mifflinburg High School and a 1994 graduate of the Pennsylvania State University with a B.S. Degree in environmental resource management. She was employed by the Pennsylvania State University for ten years in the agricultural analytical services laboratory as a supervisor of environmental testing. She was a member of the Hartley Township Recreation Committee, the Laurelton Women's Club, the Union County Sportsmen's Club, and Sacred Heart Church in Lewisburg. She died in an automobile accident.

Children: Derrick A. (*b.* 1999), Spencer A. (*b.* 2002)
[F.A.G. 99956167]

circa 1995
(permission: Kerry Wenrick)

JEAN DORA MILROY
    MRS. JOHN HERBERT AIMETTI
b. March 15, 1928, Mountain Top, Luzerne Co, PA
d. Aug. 26, 2010, Mifflinburg, Union Co, PA
bur. Hironimus Union Church Cemetery, Weikert, Union Co, PA
dau. of Lyman Derr Milroy and Crystal Viola Kirkhoff Milroy
mar. John Herbert "Jack" Aimetti, Oct. 3, 1948, Lewisburg, PA

Lived at Aimetti Lane, Weikert, PA. Jean was a bookkeeper and Air Force wife before moving to Weikert. They later moved to Tucson, Arizona. Sunday school teacher at Lincoln Chapel UMC, Laurelton, PA, for many years. They sold their property of original farm house and some grounds to Michael J. Rodarmel and Debra Shirk Rodarmel. Jack's mother, Viola Zoe Canouse Aimetti, *bur.* Hironimus Union Church Cemetery.

Children: Jeanie Lynn (*mar.* LaRue Wallace Lyons Jr., June 2, 1976), Zoe Marie (*mar.* David Michael Oldt, July 28, 1973), Crystal (*mar.* Christensen), Elizabeth Jane (*mar. 1.* Herman Lester Englehart Jr., February 25, 1974, *mar. 2.* Michael Thomas Shade, March 23, 1987, *mar. 3.* Gary Lynn Sheesley, June 1989, *mar. 4.* Ted Williams in 2016), Jo Helen (*mar.* Gasky), Jacque (*mar.* DiPalermo).

[F.A.G. 41821761]

(permission: Jeanie L. Lyons)

KATIE LEONA MINIUM
   MRS. JIMMY ROBERT ELY
b. March 24, 1938, Perry Twsp, Snyder Co, PA
d. March 8, 2016, Lewisburg, Union Co, PA
bur. Hironimus Union Church Cemetery, Weikert, Union Co, PA
dau. of Orval Minium and Sarah Feltman Minium
mar. Jimmy Robert Ely, May 4, 1963, Lewisburg, Union Co, PA
   Frequent recreational resident at 5205 Weikert Rd.
   Children: Gregg Orval Ely (*b.* June 19, 1962), Michael James Ely (*b.* Jan. 19, 1967).
   [F.A.G. 159493299]

(permission:
Jane Ely Foster)

JENNY VIRGINIA KAHLEY
    MRS. OWEN WALTER EVERETT
    MRS. CHARLES DAILEY
b. April 11, 1919
d. Dec. 9, 1995
bur. Hironimus Union Church Cemetery, Weikert, Union Co, PA
dau. of Elmer E. Kahley and Mabel Irene Barnet Kahley
mar. 1. Owen Walter "Hap" Everett
mar. 2. Charles "Red" Dailey
    "Aunt Deet" lived on Weikert Road.
    Children: Kathryn L. Everett (*mar.* Frederick).
    [F.A.G. 99956103]

(permission:
Kitty Frederick)

Women of Weikert 141

DESSIE JANE RISER
   MRS. RAY KENNETH CRONIN
b. Aug. 25, 1908, Ozark, Monroe Co, Ohio
d. July 18, 1998, Weikert, Union Co, PA
bur. Oaklawn Cemetery, Woodsfield, Monroe Co, Ohio
dau. of George F. Riser and Laura C. Shaw Riser (or Laura Ryan)
mar. Ray Kenneth Cronin (*b.* Feb. 10, 1907, in Ohio, *d.* Nov. 10, 1953, in Lewisville, Monroe Co, Ohio), Aug. 15, 1931

She lived in the house next to the store. She was a cook in various schools and an employee of the Ohio State Retirement System. Hironimus Church Memory List.

Children: Harold Robert Cronin (*b.* 1933), Paul E. Cronin (*b.* 1934, *d.* 1973).

[F.A.G. 11867183]

(permission: Toni Klauger)

JOAN E. (JANUEWSKI)
   MRS. JAMES A. JANUEWSKI
mar. James A. Januewski
   Resident in Lindale, 6515 Weikert Road, late 1990s.

Timeline of Local and National Events

1770   Hartley Township, Union County, PA, settled.

1811   Hartley Township, Union County, PA, incorporated.

1813   Union County incorporated from Northumberland County.

1813   Land records begun in Union County.

1814   March 19, Jacob Weiker's land was patented and warranted, 226 acres in the Hartleton District (Pennsylvania Warrant Register, page 312).

1824   The Hironimus family arrived.

1828   December 3: Catherine Shaffer along with George Aumiller was one of the earliest local women to have a land patent, 8 acres plus.

1829   Jacob Hironimus bought 71 acres from Mathias Snook, early patentee.

1849   Earliest known death of a Weikert woman, Mary Diehl Weiker.

1850   John Melish produced a map showing Weiker Run.

1861   April 12, United States Civil War began.

1865   May 9, United States Civil War ended.

1869   The Lindale School (the Red School) on Weikert Road began around this year.

1874   Early church and Sunday School held at the Lindale School.

1880   Hironimus School on the Weikert Road in operation; it closed in 1942.

1880   Hironimus Church completed.

1888   May 9, Bertha Louise Goodlander Bilger was the first person baptized in the Hironimus Church.

1890	Arminda Johnson Benney files a divorce petition against David Benney; divorce granted 19 years later in 1909.
1917	April 6, United States declares war on Germany.
1917	June 4: Congress passes the Woman's Suffrage Act, the 19th Amendment. It is ratified by the states in 1920.
1917	December 7, United States declares war on Austria-Hungary.
1920	The first woman was admitted to the Laurelton State Institution for Feeble-Minded Women of Child-Bearing Age. Laurelton closed in 1998.
1921	Ace Sholter opened the Weikert Store on the Weikert Road after other small local stores shut down.
1929	The Great Depression began.
1930s	Electricity comes to Weikert along the Weikert Road.
mid-1930s	The permanent concrete bridge at Weikert is built.
1939	The Jollys have telephone in Jolly's Grove.
1941	December 11, the United States declares war on Germany and Japan. Three women veterans move to Weikert following the war.
1940s	Early in the 1940s a few telephones became available.
1941	Electricity was in as far as Kortens and Snooks on Weikert Road.
1971	Television comes to Weikert Road and Jolly's Grove Lane properties via the Levan's private cable company.

Social and Economic Influences on Weikert Life

Late 1700s – The Pennsylvania government issued patents for large pieces of land, mostly with a border on Penns Creek, to Philadelphians. Then some properties were surveyed, and warrants were obtained so that many of these lands could be bought and sold. The Hayes family of Hartleton, who were surveyors, bought many of these warrants. They sold pieces to others. Early purchasers were: Goodlanders, Dorman, Hironimus, and Hendricks. Subsistence farming and woodland clearing began.

1850/60s – Maine lumbermen Libby, Marsten, Rote and Fessenden arrived to expand the lumber industry and stayed to marry local girls. According to Pardee lumbering historian Jonathan Bastian (in the *Millmont Times*, October 1, 2006), Pardee Lumber Company employed Goodlander, Aumiller, McColm, Dauberman, Pursley, Rheppart, Sholter and Barnet men and one woman with ties to Weikert, Chestia Walls.

Mid 1870s – Work on the construction of and completion of the Lewisburg to Tyrone Railroad (L. & T.) through Spring Mills and on to Bellefonte brought in men and families and gave steady employment to some of the Jolly, Koonsman, Goodlander, Johnson and Freed men. The subsequent owner, the Pennsylvania Railroad, began to petition for closure of the track in 1928. Bit by bit services were discontinued. The tracks were pulled up in 1976.

1877 – The Weikert post office opened.

1878 – The Cherry Run post office opened.

1900 – The census shows many men still employed as farmers and day laborers.

1915 – The State of Pennsylvania established the Laurelton State Village for Feeble-Minded Women of Child-Bearing Age. The first building was completed in 1917, and the first women were admitted in 1920. Local men were hired to supervise field and farm work, maintenance, and power plant labor. Many Hartley Township women and women of surrounding counties found work as cottage attendants, teachers, occupational training supervisors, and as part of the administration. Then as Pennsylvania institutions began to change in the middle to late twentieth century, Laurelton began to fade as a source for employment until its closing in 1998. It was a profound loss of income for many area families.

1933 – The Bald Eagle CCC camp opened on the J. C. Krumrine farm just east of the town center. It provided jobs for the male members of the Aumiller, Libby, Pursley, Teichman, Bilger and other families. The camp closed in 1941.

1934 – The CCC built a 143 foot concrete and steel truss bridge which was opened over Penns Creek at Weikert. The bridge allowed access to farms, camps, hunting grounds and connecting forest roads on the south side of the creek. The CCC camp veterans made major road and small bridge improvements to Weikert Road, Weikert Run Road, and Cherry Run Road. A new vehicle bridge was constructed under the Pennsylvania Railroad trestle over Cherry Run, improving access to Rt. 45, Woodward, and Penns Valley in Centre County.

Social and Economic Influences

1930s – The decade of the "Great Depression" was known as "The Dirty Thirties." The weather was severe with deep snows and extremely harsh winters, a disastrous economy, and consequent tragedies. "A time which makes our current problems nearly childish" (Kalish, *Little Heathens*).

Early 1940s – Many men and some women moved from Weikert to larger areas for war work and others car-pooled to commute to Sunbury and Milton for foundry and railroad jobs. As the lumbering and other small industries declined, the need for cabins and camps for recreation along Penns Creek and the state forest lands grew steadily and provided the opportunities for construction and other related employment for some of the men and a few women of Weikert.

1961 – The Methodist Church conference purchased the C. K. Robinson estate on the south side of Penns Creek for a church camp and conference center. The Lewisburg & Tyrone line was closed.

Bibliography

Adams, Samuel Speece, *Adams Family Ancestors, Descendants*, 1990, Sunbury, PA.

Aitkin, Gerri L., compiler, *White Springs United Methodist Church, Millmont Circuit, Union County, PA*, Lewistown, PA.

Anspach, Rev. John George, *Records 1831–1885*, Centre County Library, Bellefonte, PA.

Bastian, Jonathan, *Millmont Times*, 2006.

Bauer, Helen, *The Story of Hironimus Union Church, Weikert PA*, 1970.

The Comprehensive Plan for Union County, PA.

Cunningham, William, and Cunningham, Darla W. *Hironimus Union Church Cemetery Records.*

D'Invilliers, E. V., *Report to the State Board of Commissioners on the 2nd Geological Survey of Pennsylvania*, 1891.

Find-A-Grave, since 2007.

Genealogy of the Weiker Family (copy owned by Marion Kahley).

Haus, C. E., Dec. 9, 1875, Thomas McCurdy Interview, *Mifflinburg Telegraph*.

Hartley Township Land Owner/Tenant List 1900–1910, Union County PA Courthouse, Lewisburg, PA.

Hastings, Kate, "Medical Care," Union County Historical Society Lecture, 2017, Lewisburg. PA.

Hendricks Research Team, *Descendants of Willem Hendricks and His Sons of Montgomery Co., PA*, 2009.

Hironimus Union Church and Sunday School Records.

Jansma, Emilie Freer, *The Community of Weikert, PA – Homes and Homesteads, Cabins and Camps*, 2003.

Jansma, Emilie Freer, the compiler's personal database of *The Residents of Weikert, PA 2011*.

Kalish, Mildred Armstrong, *Little Heathens*, Bantam-Dell, 2007.

Kalp, Lois, *Silhouettes – Historic, Memorable and Notable Women of Union County, PA 1785–1985*, 1985, Lewisburg, PA.

Kline, Benjamin F. G., Jr., *Pitch Pine and Prop Timber*, Williamsport, PA, 1971.

Landis, Joyce Winn, *Hironimus Family Tree*, 2002, Halifax, PA.

Libby, Charles T., *Libby Family in America*, 1882, Maine.
Lontz, Mary Belle, *Union County Deaths, earliest to 1892, 1893–1905, 1937–1991, 1997–1998*.
Lontz, Mary Belle, *Notable Women of Union County, PA*, 2006.
Lontz, Mary Belle, *Pennsylvanians Who Went to Stephenson County, IL*.
Lontz, Mary Belle, *Union County, PA, Census Abstracts*.
Macneal, Douglas, *Centre County Heritage*, vol. 38, 2003, State College, PA.
Mayes, Dr. Donald, *Weikert, PA, Photo Collection, 2004*, Elizabethtown, PA.
Murphy, Emma M., *Wilt and Aumiller Family Book*, 2010.
O'Brien, Rita J., *Goodlander Family*, San Antonio, Texas.
O'Brien, Rita J., *Some Descendants of William P. Pursley and Eliza Switzer*, 2001, San Antonio, Texas.
Pennsylvania Department of Health, Death Certificates, accessed by Timothy Bastian.
Pennsylvania State Archives of Historical Museum Documents. 1872, Harrisburg. PA
Schneeburg, Virginia Kathryn Ely, *Reminisces (sic)* 1989.
Sheaffer, Glenda L., *Dorman Family, Descendants of Peter Dorman*, Addendum to Pearl Kaler's *Dorman History*.
Sheaffer, Glenda L., *Sholter Family*, 2005.
Shively, Tony L. and Jansma, Emilie F., *William "Papy" McColm Veteran's Records*, 2006.
Shively, Tony L. and Janice D., *The Millmont Times*, 2000–2015.
Sholter, Verna, "Weikert", *Union County Heritage*, Vol.V, 1976.
Thomas, Lowell S., *Mac/McPhersons of Pennsylvania and Related Families*, Rootsweb.
"Tight End", *Union County Heritage*, Vol. VIII, 1982.
Union County PA Deed Books, Union County Courthouse, Lewisburg, PA.
Union County PA Divorce Index 1813–. Union County Courthouse, Lewisburg, PA.
Union County PA General Marriage License Index, 1885–. Union County Courthouse, Lewisburg, PA.
Wagner, Judy Shively, *The Jacob Zimmerman, Sr. Family of Hartley Township, Union County, PA*, 2001.
West Buffalo Township Census, 1796 Excerpts, *Union County Heritage*, vol. XIV, 1994.
Winter, Raymond B., *Halfway to Winter*, 1967.

Bibliography

Wirt, Leona Sholter, *Oral History Interviews*, by Louise G. Scott, transcribed by Emilie F. Jansma.

Geographical and Thematic Index

All Saints Cemetery, Elysburg, Northumberland Co 129
Allentown, Lehigh Co 138
Altoona, Blair Co 54, 56
Alsace, France 24, 25, 26
Amsterdam, Netherlands 24
Appalachia 120
Aumiller Bottom 43, 121
Austin, Potter Co 106
Avian Haven 48, 104, 113
Baltimore, Maryland 47, 53
Beaver Springs, Snyder Co 71
Bellefonte, Centre Co 18, 51, 64, 74, 145
Bellevue Presbyterian Cemetery, Gap, Lancaster Co 92, 98, 131
Berks County 28, 86
Bethlehem, Northampton Co 49, 92, 98, 131
Bloomsburg State Normal School 64
Bloomsburg State University 126
Boltz Cemetery, Missouri 40
Bucknell University 118
Bucks Co 16, 23, 24,
Buffalo Church of the Brethren Cemetery, Mifflinburg, Union Co 79
Buffalo Twsp, Union Co 5, 26, 79, 82, 107
California 58
Canada 95
Carbon Co 54
Carlisle, Cumberland Co 7, 126
Catawissa, Columbia Co 30
Centre Co 2, 12, 14, 43, 51, 79, 90, 101, 146
Chester Co 137
Citizens Cemetery, Lavelle, Schuylkill Co 136
Coal Twsp, Northumberland Co 108, 129
Coatesville, Chester Co 137
Cochran Field, Georgia 130

Compassville, Chester Co 131
Cressona, Schuylkill Co 129
Danville, Montour Co 12, 30, 97, 103, 125, 134
Dauphin Cemetery, Harrisburg, Dauphin Co 99
Deptford, London, England 123
Doylestown Cemetery, Bucks Co 71
Dunbar, Fayette Co 123
Durham, Connecticut 133
East Buffalo Twsp, Union Co 82, 107
East Side Cemetery, Mifflinburg, Union Co 107
East Stroudsburg State Teachers' College 116
East Stroudsburg University 126
Easton, Northampton Co 112
Ebensburg, Cambria Co 86
Evangelical United Brethren Cemetery, Belsano, Cambria Co 62
Forty Fort, Luzerne Co 117
Franklin, Venango Co 120
Franklin Cemetery, Franklin, Venango Co 120
Franklin Heights Memorial Park, E. Weissport, Carbon, Co 54
Germany 24, 25, 26, 44
Glaus Haus 116
Glaze Twsp, Miller Co, Missouri 27
Glen Iron, Union Co 40, 56, 93
Grace Evangelical Church Cemetery, Laurelton, Union Co 39
Hagerstown, Maryland 129, 134
Haines Twsp, Centre Co 69, 97, 138
Harmony Cemetery, Milton, Northumberland Co 69, 85, 121
Harrisburg, Dauphin Co 80, 99, 121, 126, 129
Hartleton, Union Co 24, 32, 49, 51, 91, 103, 107, 113, 118, 123, 130, 143, 145
Hartleton Cemetery, Union Co 46, 48, 49, 51, 52, 58, 72, 112, 114, 119, 125,

127, 135
Hartley Twsp, Union Co 2, 5, 6, 9, 10, 23, 27, 32, 39, 40, 42, 44, 48, 55, 61, 66, 71, 73, 76, 79, 82, 83, 96, 99, 103, 105, 106, 107, 113, 117, 121, 138, 143, 146
Hedrick Cemetery, East Conemaugh, Cambria Co 65
Highland Cemetery, New Columbia, Union Co 103
Hillview Cemetery, Greensburg, Westmoreland Co 123
Hironimus Union Church Cemetery, Weikert, Union Co 23, 28, 30, 31, 32, 36, 39, 40, 41, 43, 44, 45, 46, 47, 49, 52, 55, 56, 58, 59, 61, 62, 63, 65, 66, 69, 71, 73, 74, 75, 76, 77, 78, 79, 82, 83, 84, 86, 87, 88, 89, 91, 93, 94, 95, 96, 98, 99, 100, 101, 102, 104, 107, 110, 113, 117, 118, 124, 126, 128, 129, 130, 132, 134, 137, 138, 139, 140
Hollidaysburg, Blair Co 125
Holsapple, Somerset Co 72
Hope Mills, North Carolina 124
Hummelstown Cemetery, Dauphin Co 51
Huntersville Webster Cemetery, Lycoming Co 121
Huntingdon Co 13, 101
Huntingdon, West Virginia 54
Jack's Mountain, Union Co 87
Jamestown, Chatauqua Co, New York 109-110
Jefferson Medical College School of Nursing 118
Johnstown, Cambria Co 62, 67
Jolly's Grove 86, 144
Juniata Co 31
Juniata Memorial Cemetery, Lewistown, Mifflin Co 105
Kansas 40, 59
Keister Cemetery, Weikert, Union, Co 25, 26, 29, 33, 34, 35, 38, 50, 54, 57, 59, 81
Kelly Twsp, Union Co 72
Kentucky 33

Lakeview Cemetery, Jamestown, Chatauqua Co, New York 106
Laurelton 7, 10, 11, 12, 13, 14, 19, 30, 32, 36, 46, 49, 52, 58, 63, 64, 72, 81, 89, 90, 91, 92, 96, 98, 99, 102, 103, 107, 113, 114, 118, 119, 120, 121, 122, 127, 130, 135, 138, 139, 144, 146
Laurelton State Village employee 89, 91, 92, 96, 98, 114, 118, 119, 122, 127, 135
Laurelton Women's Club 113, 119, 120, 130, 135, 138
Lavelle, Schuylkill Co 136
Lewis Twsp, Snyder Co 46
Lewis Twsp, Union Co 45, 67, 90, 112
Lewisburg, Union Co 12, 55, 62, 63, 65, 67, 69, 72, 73, 87, 88, 89, 91, 95, 96, 100, 101, 103, 103, 107, 114, 115, 118, 119, 120, 124, 128, 130, 132, 134, 135, 136, 138, 139, 145
Lewisburg Cemetery, Lewisburg, Union Co 57, 104
Lewistown, Mifflin Co 40, 84
Lewisville, Monroe Co, Ohio 141
Lincoln Chapel, Laurelton, Union Co 27, 28, 37, 42, 47, 48, 68, 80, 90, 108, 115, 130
Long Lane Cemetery, Laurelton, Union Co 43, 60, 64, 89, 91, 93, 96, 101
Lowell School Cemetery, Seneca Co, Ohio 24
Luzerne Co 60, 126
Madera, Clearfield Co 133
Maine 38, 145
Maryland 33, 34, 52
McAlisterville, Juniata Co 56
McKeesport, Allegheny Co 121
Middleburg, Snyder Co 61, 77, 78, 100
midwife 31, 53
Mifflinburg, Union Co 10, 24, 35, 73, 91, 106, 122, 123, 129, 138
Mifflin Co 32, 61, 65
Miller Co, Missouri 27, 40
Millerstown, Perry Co 104, 112
Millmont, Union Co 45, 49, 65, 66, 67, 73, 86, 88, 103, 111, 114, 117, 130,

Geographical Index

132, 135
Milroy, Mifflin Co 31, 32, 84
Milton, Northumberland Co 48, 85, 91, 103
Missouri 7, 40
Moreland Cemetery, Wayne Co, Ohio 23
Mt. Holyoke College 133
Mountain Grove Cemetery, Luzerne Co 72
New Berlin Cemetery, Union Co 42, 134
Mountain Top, Luzerne Co 138
Muncy, Lycoming Co 108, 113
Nahanne 87
Nanty-Glo, Cambria Co 118
New Berlin, Union Co 30, 48, 64, 76, 125, 134
New Columbia, Union Co 102
New Cumberland 127
New Jersey 33, 37
Newark, New Jersey 132
Northampton Memorial Shrine, Easton, Northampton Co 112
Northumberland Co 28
Northumberland Memorial Park, Stonington, Northumberland Co 111
Oaklawn Cemetery, Woodsfield, Ohio 141
Ohio 7, 23, 76, 141
Oil City, Venango Co 49, 65
Old Cedars Cemetery, Swengel, Union Co 45, 67, 90
Old Fellows Cemetery, Shamokin, Northumberland Co 70
Oldtown, Maryland 74, 107, 135
Orangeville, Columbia Co 73
Orwigsburg, Schuylkill Co 128
Ozark, Monroe Co, Ohio 141
Pardee, Union Co 2, 3, 16, 19, 46, 61, 74, 110, 120, 145
Pardee Station, Union Co 36
Patch Grove, Wisconsin 43
Pennsylvania, University of 67
Pennsylvania State University 138
Perry Twsp, Snyder Co 139
Philadelphia 6, 46, 87, 99, 130, 136
Pine Acres 92, 98, 131

Pine Grove Twsp, Schuylkill Co 128, 129
Pittsburgh 133
Pleasant Grove, Union Co 91, 106
Pocohontas, West Virginia 54
Pomfret Manor Cemetery, Northumberland Co 125
postmaster 16, 53, 59, 68, 118, 124
quilter 5, 15, 90, 110, 120, 136
Reedsville, Mifflin Co 94, 105
Ridgeway, Elk Co 16
Rochester, New York 135
Rockefeller Twsp, Northumberland Co 134
Rock Glen, Luzerne Co 72
Rosehill Cemetery, Altoona, Blair Co 56
Roselle, New Jersey 133
St. Peter's Reformed Church Cemetery, Paxinos, Northumberland Co 122
St. Peter's Church Cemetery, Pine Grove Twsp, Schuylkill Co 128
St. Peter's Church Cemetery (Ray's Church), Union Co 26, 81, 109
Scranton, Lackawanna Co 104
Selinsgrove, Snyder Co 134-5
Silver Spring Twsp, Cumberland Co 62
Shamokin, Northumberland Co 67, 70, 115-16, 132
Snyder Co 93
State College, Centre Co 103
Sunbury, Northumberland Co 12, 17, 100, 104, 107, 108, 111, 113, 123, 125, 130, 147
Tennessee 120
Three Springs, Huntingdon Co 101
Tin Shanty 92
Troxelville Union Cemetery, Snyder Co 44
Tucson, Arizona 139
Uhrwiller, Alsace, France 24
Union Cemetery, Woodward, Centre Co 97
Union County Spotsmen's Club 48, 97, 120, 125, 126, 134, 138
Vintondale, Cambria Co 118
Walnut Hill Farm 92, 98, 131

Ward Memorial Cemetery, Brookings, Oregon 121
Warfordsburg, Fulton Co 115
Watsontown, Northumberland Co 82, 105, 130
Watsontown Cemetery, Northumberland Co 129
Waynesboro, Franklin Co 127
West Buffalo Twsp, Union Co 5, 26
West Chester State Teacher's College 126
West Side Cemetery, Shamokin Dam, Snyder Co 123
Wharton, Potter Co 59
White Springs UMC Circuit 7-8, 31, 32, 36, 38, 43, 46, 48, 51, 52, 53, 54, 55, 57, 58, 59, 63, 64, 68, 69, 73, 75, 77, 79, 83, 85, 88, 95, 97, 109, 117, 119
Williamsport, Lycoming Co 112, 118
Winfield, Union Co 55, 78
Winthrop, Massachusetts 137
Wisconsin, University of 133
Woodmere Memorial Park, Huntingdon, West Virginia 53

Index of Personal Names

Acker, Agnes Sophia 107
Ackerman, Adam, *mar.* Catherine Hironimus 24, 25
Adams, Floyd 124
– Jean Howell (1929–2014), *mar.* Joseph Roland Sholter 124
Aikey, Agnes Jane (1855–1921), *mar.* Benjamin F. Sholter 51
– Anna M. 112
– Thomas J. 51
Aimetti, Crystal, *mar.* Christensen 139
– Elizabeth Jane, *mar. 1.* Herman Lester Englehart, *mar. 2.* Michael Thomas Shade, *mar. 3.* Gary Lynn Sheesley, *mar. 4.* Ted Williams 139
– Jacque, *mar.* DiPalermo 139
– Jeanie Lynn, *mar.* LaRue Wallace Lyons 139
– Jo Helen, *mar.* Gasky 139
– John Herbert, *mar.* Jean Dora Milroy 138-9
– Zoe Marie, *mar.* David Michael Oldt 139
Albright, Barbara, *mar.* Jesse Hendricks 23
– Frederick 23
Alexander, Preston B., *mar.* Isabelle Bertha Jolly 73
Allen, Daisy 80
Ammon, William Earl, *mar.* Helen Neuhauser 92
Arbogast, Helen E. 75
Auchmuty, Lucinda 49
Aumiller, Aaron A. 43
– Ada E., *mar.* Katherman 43
– Anna (1843/51–1919), *mar.* William F. Johnson 30, 40-1
– Bertha Elsie, mar. Fetterolf 44
– Carbon Cleveland 44
– Carrie Mabel, mar. Lepley 44
– Catherine Elizabeth, mar. Folk 44
– Cleveland Manassah 93

– Crawford C. 30
– Flora, *mar.* Gill 44
– George J. 40
– George Michael Jr., *mar.* Sarah Hartman 30
– George Washington, *mar.* Catherine Galer 30
– Gertrude, *mar.* Dorman 43
– Harriet, *mar.* Boop 43
– Hattie Mabel, *mar.* Renn 30
– Isabell Ann (1878–1913), *mar.* Samuel Conrad Wilt 84, 93
– James 30
– Jeremiah 30
– John David 44
– Lavina, *mar.* Carpenter 30
– Mary Jane (1869–1894), *mar.* John E. Rheppard 30, 45
– Manassah T., *mar.* Sarah Agnes Badger 30
– Mary Jane 44
– Mary Normatta (1883–1910), *mar.* Daniel Cherry 93, 94
– Michael William 30
– Percival, *mar.* Mina/Mena Henry 30, 43
– Sarah Mae, mar. Sipe 44
– Wesley 43
– William 44
– Williamson Washington 93
Auten, Joan Maxine (1935–2006) 125
– John M. 125
Badger, Bob 85
– Sarah Agnes (1862/63–1952), *mar.* Manassah T. Aumiller 85, 94
Bailey, see Dorman, Miriam A.
Barker, Anne 88
– Cora C. (c. 1875–1943), *mar.* William W. Koonsman 90, 109
– Frank P. 90
Barnet, Dora Jane 82
– Edward Earl 73

Barnet, Edward T., *mar.* Barbara Louise Pavelic 126
– Eva 40
– George O., *mar.* Mary Elizabeth Sholter 26, 40
– Jacob, *mar.* Catherina Weiker 23
– Jacob F., *mar.* Catherine Shirk 26, 41
– James 26
– John, *mar.* Eva Hironimus 23
– John H. 41
– John M. 40
– Jonas William, *mar.* Isabelle Bertha Jolly 73, 82
– Lucy J. 40
– Simon Henry 40
– Thomas J. 40
– William F., *mar.* Lily E. Jordan 41, 82
Barnett, August 88
– Barbara Ruth (1934–2016), *mar.* Harold R. Cronin 113
– Benjamin 74
– Blanche M. 74
– Cora 88
– Daisey 74
– Freda Joyce, *mar.* Barker 102
– Irene M., *mar.* Hill 87, 102
– Jacob Charles, *mar. 1.* Amber Mae Bettilyon, *mar. 2.* Blanche Pursley, *mar. 3.* Edna Mae Middlesworth, *mar. 4.* (Margaretta) Kathryn Geyer 86-7, 102
– Jacob W. 74
– John, *mar.* Elizabeth Jenkins 62
– John H., *mar.* Mary E. Sholter 74
– Jonas Franklin 88
– Jonas W., *mar.* Virginia Gertrude Libby 88
– L. Jane, *mar.* Strickler 88
– Mabel Irene (1899–1971), *mar.* Elmer Elsworth Kahley 74
– William D. 87, 102
Bartley, Clara E. (c. 1884–1957), *mar.* Edward L. Sholter 99-100
– Henry 99
– Kate 128
Bastian, see Wirt, Connie

Bauer, August Karl, *mar.* Jessie Helen Bickel 87
– James A. 87
– L. George 87
– Richard C. 87
– Robert E. 87
Baylor, Bailor
– Arabel 60
– William, *mar.* Sarah Libby 60
– William 60
Beaver, J. Raymond 122
– Jane Elizabeth (1917–1997), *mar.* Donald L. Kline 122
Beck, Warren 127
Bennett, see Bettilyon, Mary M.
– Rose 77
Benney, also Benny, Binney
– Annie A. (1869–1918), *mar. 1.* Henry Buffington, *mar. 2.* Frank Boop 47, 54
– David, *mar.* Arminda Johnson 47, 52, 54, 57, 65, 83
– Catherine V. 54-5
– Ida, *mar.* Reid 55
– Joseph Cees 55
– Laura, *mar.* Wikel 55
– MaryBelle, *mar.* Rearick 54
– Minnie, *mar.* Fuhrman 55
– Sarah Alice (1876–1959), *mar.* Oliver Catherman 52, 55
Benson, Henry 83
Berkstressor, Edwin 33
– Jacob 33
– Joseph 33
– Margaret 33
– Phoebe 33
– Stewart 33
Bettilyon, also Bettlyon, Bethlehem, Bettelyon, Bithelon
– Amber Mae (1903/04–1927/28), *mar.* Jacob Charles Barnett 69
– Ambrose, *mar.* Sarah Jane Jolly 49
– Ambrose 94
– Ambrose D., *mar.* Margaret J. Tate 57, 68-9, 87
– Aramindi 94

Index of Personal Names

Bettilyon, Barbara 88
– George Edward 69
– Geraldine 88
– Guy Alvin 69
– Ida 88
– James Lester, *mar.* Virginia Gertrude Libby 69
– Jennie 69
– Lester 88
– Mary E. 69
– Mary M., *mar.* Bennett 77
– Mary M., *mar.* Alvah W. Longer 57
– Rhoda E. G. or Rodastella 69
– William O. 69
Bickel, George Washington 87
– Jessie Helen (1897–1983), *mar.* August Karl Bauer 87
Bilger, Benjamin James 108
– Caroline, *mar.* Wenrick 101
– Carrie 93
– Charles 93
– David 108
– Doris 53
– George H. 101
– George W. 93
– George William, *mar.* Ruth Ann Wilson 101
– Gertrude Bertha 108
– Helen C. 53
– James, Sr., *mar.* Bertha Louise Goodlander 52-3
– James D. 93
– James Daniel 53
– Jim 108
– June, *mar.* Tyson 101
– Laura, *mar.* E. Kauffman Rishel 101
– Leona 53
– Lottie 93
– Lottie, *mar.* Brown 101
– Martha V. 53
– Mary 93
– Maude E. 53
– Maudella 93
– May 53
– Paul 93
– Pauline, *mar.* Thompson 101
– Robert, Jr., *mar.* Marguerite Cressinger 108
– Robert E. or B. 53
– Robert Franklin, *mar.* Harriet Susanna Bogar 93
– Roberta Pauline 108
– Rose 53
– Wilson E. 101
Bingaman, Daniel J. 63
– Earl M. 63
– Everitt V. 63
– Frederick 33
– Gladys Geraldine (1911–2004), *mar.* Floyd Washington Harvey 117
– Glydia Geraldine 63
– Isabel Virginia 63
– Mary Lou 63
– Rhoda Mae 63
– Ruth Aletta 63
– Simon Frederick 63
– Simon Showalter, *mar.* Cora Louise Sholter 63, 77, 117
– William Orvis 63
Bitner, Albert Newton, *mar.* Rosa Louisa Goodlander 48, 81
Blankenship, J. M., *mar.* Arminda Johnson 53
Bloom, George 124
Blyler, Ellen S. 72
– Mamie Willowfern 114
Bogar, Daniel J. 93
– Harriet Susanna (1858–1930), *mar.* Robert Franklin Bilger 93
Bohnestiel, William, *mar.* Catherine Shively 35
Bolich, John 59
Boob, Catherine 37
– Daniel 37
– Elizabeth 37
– James 37
– John 37
– Julian 37
– Lydia 37
– Margaret 37
– Mary, *mar.* Michael Boob 37
– Michael, *mar.* Mary 37

Boob, Samuel 37
– Sarah 37
– William 37
Boop, see Aumiller, Harriet
– see Johnson, Minnie Elizabeth May
– see Pursley, Clara A.
– Charles 58
– Cora 41
– Frank, *mar.* Annie A. Benney 47
– John, *mar.* Sarah Jane Jolly 49
– Laura Alice, *mar.* Feaster 47
– Mary Aumiller (1869–1894), *mar.* John E. Rheppard 45, 95
Border, Ethel, *mar.* Elmer J. Keister 104
Bower, see Yocum, Carole J.
Bowersox, see Johnson, Nellie Viola
– David 58
Boyer, see Libby, Jean L.
Bracken, also Brachen
– Belle 86
– Mary Blanche (1876–1964), *mar.* Edward Thomas Jolly 73, 86, 89
– John (or Davis) 86
Bridge, Alice, *mar.* George Bridge 53
– Edward 57
– George 53
– George, *mar.* Margaret, Mary 57
– Hannah/Mary (1862–1945), *mar.* Henry F. Dorman 45, 86
– Jacob 57
– Jeremiah 53
– Lewis 57
– Margaret 57
– Margaret, *mar.* George Bridge 57
– Mary 53
– Mary 57
– Mary Ann (1859–1920), *mar.* William H. Bridge 57
– Merrit 57
– Sarah 67
– William H., *mar.* Mary Ann Bridge 57
Briggman, see Silvius, Miriam R.
Brouse, Harold 60
– Helen 60
– Lawrence, *mar.* Sarah Libby 60, 64
– William 60

Brown, see Bilger, Lottie
– Charles 50
Bruss, Abraham 81
– Annie S. (1870–1932), *mar.* (John) Charles Bruss 81
– Clarence D. 81
– Elmer Isaac 81
– (John) Charles, *mar.* Annie S. 81
– Kate 81
– Mary 81
– Oscar F. 81
Buffington, David James 47
– Edward 78
– Edward Lewis 47
– Elizabeth Minerva (1859–1929), *mar.* George Washington Sholter 54, 78
– Harry A. 47
– Henry, *mar.* Annie A. Benney 47
– William Reno 47
Burd, Hannah (c. 1799–1860), *mar.* Jacob Hironimus Jr. 24-5
Burkman, Conrad R. 131
– Armena Elizabeth (1895–1990), *mar.* Robert Leroy Neuhauser 131
Burns, George 50
– Lucy (1840–1920), *mar.* Andrew Hironimus 25, 44, 49-50, 64, 69, 70, 91
Buswell, see Jordan, Tracy
Caldwell, see Libby, Ethel R.
Callahan, Pansy A. (1930–2016), *mar.* Richard W. Jordan 123
– Thomas 123
Campbell, Maude Louise 134
Canouse, also Knauss
– Jacob Edward 112
– Marian Rosella (*d.* 1895), *mar.* John Russell Libby 112
– Violet Zoe 139
Cardin, Catherine 136
– Clarence 110
Catherman, see also Katherman
– see Dorman, Grace Margaret
– Calvin 25
– Elvina or Lavina 51
– Grace Mathilda, *mar.* Folk 52
– Harold Thomas 52

Index of Personal Names

Catherman, Hattie 25
– John 52
– Oliver, *mar.* Sarah Alice Benney 52, 54
– Susan 52
Cherry, Charles E. 94
– Daniel, *mar.* Mary Normatta Aumiller 94
– Morrison Darlington 94
Christensen, see Aimetti, Crystal
Clark, Harriet (1868–1956), *mar.* Oscar Reed Goodlander 52, 76, 80-1
– Sylvester S. 81
Clifford, see Dauberman, Clair
Clyde, Annie 137
Clymer, Barbara, *mar.* Henry Hendricks 24
Codling, Alice Ethel (1896–1953) 123
– Elijah John 123
Colyer, see Himmelreich, Mary
Cook, C. D. 59
Cooney, Catherine Delores (1918–2009), *mar.* Lewis W. Klauger 136
– Richard 136
Corbin, Selena Isabelle (1847–1898), *mar.* Theodore Freed 61, 65, 83
Crebs, Paul S. 111
– Pauline A. (1929–2015), *mar.* William E. Levan Jr. 111
Cressinger, Marguerite (1916–2012), *mar.* Robert B. Bilger Jr. 108
– Royal 108
Cromly, William 39
Cronin, Harold R., *mar.* Barbara Ruth Barnett 113
– Chivi Marie, *mar.* Dagg 113
– Harold Robert 141
– Lyman Ray 113
– Michelle Ann 113
– Patrick Erin 113
– Paul E. 141
– Ray Kenneth, *mar.* Dessie Jane Riser 141
Crouse, see Pursley, Mary Ellen
Custer, Roy 83
Dagg, see Cronin, Chivi Marie

Dailey, Charles, *mar.* Virginia J. Kahley 140
Dauberman, Arthur C. 95
– Betty 95
– Clair, *mar.* Clifford 95
– Dorothy Jane, *mar.* Good 95
– Elmer Reno, *mar.* Estella Elizabeth Reppert 45, 95
– Gerald L. 95
– John R. 95
– Olive Mae 95
– P. Jean 95
Deal (Diehl), Frederick 24
– Mary (1774–1849), *mar.* Jacob Weiker 24
Derr, Amanda Christine (1844–1934), *mar.* Jacob Franklin Spacht 60-1
– Andrew 70
Dersham, Elizabeth 35
DiPalermo, see Aimetti, Jacque
Dorman, see Aumiller, Gertrude
– Charles 114
– Daniel Lawrence 67
– David 67
– George 67
– Grace Margaret, *mar.* Catherman 67
– Henry F., *mar.* Hannah/Mary Bridge 45, 59, 67, 86
– Lewis Ellsworth 67
– Lincoln 67
– Luther 67
– Minnie (1862/1888–1941), *mar.* Edward Embeck 45, 67
– Miriam A., *mar.* Bailey 67
– Samuel Peter 67
– Vada P. 103
– William 67
Drumheller, Melvin 124
Eckrod, Don 70
– Jeanne 70
Edberg, Evald G., *mar.* Hazel Munson? 106, 109
– Janet (1928–1992?), *mar.* George J. Sholter Sr. 106, 110
Egnew, see Wintersteen, Ginger
Eisenhuth, Thomas H., *mar.* Jennie

Virginia Quinlan 68
Ely, Amelia 123
– David 96
– Gregg Orval 139
– Jane Amelia, *mar.* Paul Foster 114, 123
– Jimmy Robert, *mar.* Katie Leona Minium 114, 139
– Kenneth 107
– Mary Etta (1875–1968), *mar.* David Crawford Johnson 96
– Michael James 139
– Robert Kermit, *mar.* Amelia Jane Kaler 114
– Robert M. 127
– Virginia Kathryn (1912–2009), *mar.* Max Schneeberg 107, 118
– William Allen 127
– William David, *mar.* Natalie Joann Harne 127
– William Henry 118
Embeck, Edward, *mar.* Minnie Dorman 45, 67
Engle, Jay A. 116
– Jeff B. 116
– Jere L., *mar.* Mary Lou Kline 115
– Jere L., Jr. 116
Englehart, Herman Lester 139
Engleman, John 125
– Virginia Mae (1920–1982), *mar.* Franklin B. Steese 125
Erdley, Eunice M., *mar.* Richard Swain 103
– Jerome 100
– Miles D. 103
– Myron Leon, *mar.* Jean Howell Adams 124
– Ruth Denise 103
– Verna Theora (1890–1982), *mar.* Asa Roland Sholter 100, 103, 107, 111
Everett, Kathryn L., *mar.* Frederick 140
– Owen W., *mar.* Virginia J. Kahley 97, 140
Farrow, Kimber C., *mar.* Ruth Viola Sholter 70, 71
Feaster, see Boop, Laura Alice
Feese, Rachel 82

Feibig, Mary C. 129
Feltman, Sarah 139
Fessenden, James Lemuel 42
– Philip C., *mar.* Maria Sarah Louisa Goodlander 42
Fetterolf, see Aumiller, Bertha Elsie
Fidunak, Tilka 132
File, Alfred 51
Folk, see Aumiller, Catherine Elizabeth
Folk, see Catherman, Grace Mathilda
Foltz 87
Foster, Paul 114
– Paul Michael 114
Fox, Chester Rea 90
Frederick, see Everett, Kathryn L.
– Alice, *mar.* Charles Boop 58
– Samuel 58
Freed, Abraham, *mar.* Mary Ann Saxton 62
– Ellen 50
– Ida Seymour (1868–1938), *mar. 1.* Daniel Carey Libby Sr., *mar. 2.* James Libby 61-2, 65, 88, 91
– Mary Ellen (1873–1930), *mar.* John William Hironimus 65, 66, 72, 75, 83
– Theodore, *mar.* Selena Isabelle 61, 83
– Theodore, *mar.* Arminda Johnson 53, 56, 62
– William M. 62
Friggle, Genevieve (1903–1994), *mar.* Earl P. Weaser 120
– Mattie Maud 120
– William 120
Fuhrman, see Benney, Minnie
Galer, see also Gahler, Kaler
– Andrew 27
– Carbon 74
– Caroline 43
– Carrie 79
– Catherine (1854–1928), *mar.* George Washington Aumiller 32
– Charles 84
– Charles Newton 71
– Charles W., *mar.* Alice Catherine Shields 51
– Daniel, *mar.* Elizabeth 27
– David, *mar.* Jane Parsons 43, 59

Index of Personal Names

Galer, David. *mar.* Sara 84
– David C., *mar.* Mary Catherine McPherson 32, 39
– David P., *mar.* Cora Bella McPherson 71
– Edward C., *mar.* Irene Elizabeth Staudinger 110
– Elizabeth 43
– Elizabeth, *mar. 1.* Daniel Galer, *mar. 2.* Laurenz Hendricks 27
– Elizabeth, *mar.* Alvah Marston Jr. 32, 59
– Ethel, *mar.* Palensar 62
– Florence 62
– George 44
– Harry J. 79
– Hazel 79
– Howard 62
– Jacob C. 32
– James 84
– James W. 71
– John, *mar.* Jane Switzer 27, 31
– John H., *mar.* Elizabeth Jenkins 62, 118
– John M. 44, 62
– John W. 32
– Margaret 61
– Margaret 27
– Margaret Adele (1889–1922), *mar.* James McCellan Hironimus 61, 74, 135
– Mary 27
– Mary A. 32
– Michael 27
– Michael 43
– Nancy 52
– Nora 62
– Sara, *mar.* David Galer 84
– Sara, *mar.* Sholter 62
– Sarah Jane 43
– Sarah L. (1918–1997), *mar.* George J. Sholter Sr. 118
– Thomas 79
– Zachary T., *mar. 1.* Sarah Elizabeth A. C. Goodlander, *mar. 2.* Phoebe Styers? 30, 32, 43-4, 57, 80, 110
Gasky, see Aimetti, Jo Helen

Gaston, Martin 127
– Maryann, *mar.* Losik 127
– Michael S., *mar.* Barbara Louise Pavelic 126
Geyer, Edward 102
– (Margaretta) Kathryn (1905–1998), *mar.* Jacob Charles Barnett 102
Gill, see Aumiller, Flora
Glaus, James, *mar.* Violet May Pearson 116
– Jeff 116
– Scott 116
– William 116
Glover, see Pursley, Aminda
– Louise 133
Goehring, Louise (1937–1997), *mar.* James Scott 133
– Raymond 133
Good, see Dauberman, Dorothy Jane
Goodlander, Albert 81, 109
– Amber M. (1916–2007) 101
– Benjamin 23, 27, 28
– Benjamin Thomas. *mar.* Velma Nadine Layton 81
– Bertha Louise (1888–1976), *mar.* James Bilger Sr. 81
– Bessie H., *mar.* Lundgren 81
– Catherine (1810–1884), *mar.* John E. Sholter 28
– Christian or Christopher 28, 42, 43
– Christian, *mar.* Elizabeth Wertz (Wuerz) 28
– Christopher, *mar.* Jane E. Goodlander 30
– Daniel Roy, *mar.* Lottie Keller 68
– Eliza (1813–1886), *mar.* Jacob Shirk 29
– Harriet, *mar.* Snyder 81
– Jacob 68
– James 68
– Jamilla (1848–1895), *mar.* William Eckley Weikel 28, 42
– Jane E., *mar.* Christopher Goodlander 30, 43
– Jeremiah Warren 68
– John 68
– John D., *mar.* Margaret 28, 33

Goodlander, John Leroy C., *mar. 1.*
Mary C. Pursley, *mar. 2.* Jennie
Virginia Quinlan 81
– Margaret, *mar.* John D. Goodlander
28, 33
– Maria Sarah Louisa (1842–1903), *mar.*
Philip C. Fessenden 42
– Martha 28
– Mary 30
– Mary Elizabeth (1796–1880), *mar.*
Benjamin Goodlander 28
– Nancy 30
– Newton Bitner 81
– Oscar Reed, *mar.* Harriet Clark 31, 40, 52, 80-1
– Rebecca 68
– Rosa Louisa (1874–1951), *mar.* Albert Newton Bitner 48, 68
– Sarah Elizabeth A. C. (1847/57–1925), *mar.* Zachary T. Galer 43-4
Gouchnour, Bessie A. 130
Greene, Harold 104
– Harry Jefferson, *mar.* Anna Minerva Weller 103
– Joyce 104
– June 104
Grubb, Charles E. 56
– Perry L., *mar.* Elizabeth Hostetler 56
Haas, see Pursley, Molly
Haines, Olive Neiman 130
Halley, see Wintersteen, Linda
Hanselman, Carl E. 134
– P. Joan (1940–2007), *mar.* Orville L. Spangler 134-5
Harne, Norris Allen 127
– Natalie Joann (1927–2002), *mar.* William David Ely 127
Hartman 66
– Hannah (1786–1864?), *mar.* John Hartman 33
– John, *mar.* Hannah 33
– Mary 30
– Sarah (1825–1890), *mar.* George Michael Aumiller 30, 40, 45
– William 30
Harvey, Betty L. 117

– Daniel Robert 117
– David Wayne 117
– Floyd Earl 117
– Floyd Washington, *mar.* Gladys Geraldine Bingaman 63, 117
– Galen William 117
– Kathryn E. 117
– Richard James 117
– Terry Lee 117
Hassinger, O. or Alfred P. 79
– Nancy Rebecca (1863–1938), *mar.* William J. Hironimus 25, 79, 105
Havice, Heidelinde 124
Helwig, *mar.* Pursley, Eliza
Hendricks, Abraham, *mar.* Hannah 27, 33
– Hannah (c. 1800–1869), *mar.* Abraham Hendricks 27, 33
– Henry, *mar.* Barbara Clymer 24
– Jesse, *mar.* Barbara Albright 23
– Laurenz, *mar.* Elizabeth (Gahler/Galer) 27
– Mary 23
– Nathaniel 27
Henry, Mina/Mena (1848/49–1930), *mar.* Percival Aumiller 43
Hile, Clement 130
– Rhoda Jeanette (1910–1997), *mar.* Robert Omer Curtis Kline 130
Hill, see Barnett, Irene M.
Himmelreich, Anna Linn 125
– April, *mar.* Yost 125
– Carol 125
– Dale 125
– Jackie 125
– L. Roy, *mar.* Thelma Lamey 125
– L. Roy, Jr. 125
– Mary, *mar.* Colyer 125
– Nathan 125
Hironimus, also Hieronumis
– Albert Valentine 83
– Andrew, *mar.* Lucy Burns 25, 50, 91
– Andrew James, *mar.* Bertha Rote 50
– Annie Elizabeth (1868–1912), *mar.* James Libby 50
– Annie M. 79

Index of Personal Names 165

Hironimus, Argyle E. 75
– Bessie Margaret (1890–1967), *mar.* Ammon John Shaffer 83, 98
– Catherine (1798–1874), *mar.* Adam Ackerman 24, 25
– Catherine, *mar.* Catherman 25
– Catherine 83
– Cecil J., *mar.* Helen E. Arbogast 75
– Charles F., *mar.* Amelia Jones 83
– Charlotte 79
– Charlotte May (1882–1967), *mar. 1.* John Irwin, *mar. 2.* George Lincoln Zechman 50, 90-1
– Elizabeth 25
– Ellen B., *mar.* Emmett Weiand 50
– Eva (1807–1877), *mar.* John Barnet 26
– Eva May 83
– Eva Regina (1873–1946), *mar.* Frank Seymore Jolly 50, 69, 85
– Franklin Perry 50
– George Burns, *mar.* Annie Minerva Kleckner 50, 82
– George F. 83
– Guy R., *mar. 1.* Florence Savage, *mar. 2.* Catherine 83
– Hannah Jane, *mar.* Alvin Boop 50
– Hilda, *mar.* James Leasure 75
– Ida Bell 50
– Ida C. (1898–1963), *mar.* Leon Harrison Miller 72, 83
– Jacob, Sr., *mar.* Eva Zeiter 26
– Jacob, Jr., *mar.* Hannah Burd 24
– James McCellan, *mar.* Margaret Adele Galer 79, 135
– John 25
– John W., *mar.* Mabel Jones 83
– John William, *mar.* Mary Ellen Freed 50, 62, 66, 72, 75, 83
– Kathryn (1877–1945), *mar.* John Benjamin Sholter 50, 70
– Laura K. 83
– Lucy B., *mar.* Roy Custer 83
– Mabel Emma 83
– Margaretha (1806–1879), *mar.* Christian Shaffer 26
– Mark E., *mar.* Odessa Watkins 83

– Mary 25
– Mary Lucinda (1862–1887), *mar.* James L. Libby 44-5, 50
– Mildred F. (1909–1999), *mar.* Charles W. Teichman 75, 135
– Mildred Rose, *mar.* Henry Benson 83
– Myrtle Rae, *mar.* Bruce Schnure 75
– Ruth May (1900–1944), *mar.* William Pursley 83
– Samuel H. 79
– Samuel Jacob 50
– Sarah Alice, *mar.* Charles Brown 50
– Sarah Anna, *mar.* Marlin Kenee 75
– Sarah E. (1894–1986), *mar.* Daniel C. Libby Jr. 79
– William J., *mar.* Nancy Rebecca Hassinger 25
– William J., Jr. 79
Hoffman 71
Hosterman, Thomas William 97
– Tome Elverta (1876–1941), *mar.* John C. Krumrine 48, 97
Hostetler, David 56
– Elizabeth (c. 1854–1937), *mar.* Perry L. Grubb 56
Howell, Alberta 124
Hoy, Helen M. 115
Hughes, Pansy 123
Hunter, Charles J., *mar.* Mary Hunter 38
– Franklin 38
– Joseph H. 38
– Mary, *mar.* Charles J. Hunter 38
– Sarah J. 38
Irwin, Esther W., *mar.* Shipper 91
– John, *mar.* Charlotte Hironimus 91
– John L. 91
– Kathryn E., *mar.* Gordon G. Fritz 91
– Pauline L., *mar.* Ely 91
– Susan Alice (1903–1979), *mar.* Arthur J. Kreps 90, 91
– Therlow B. 91
Januewski, James A., Jr., *mar.* Joan E. 141
– Joan E., *mar.* James A. Januewski Jr. 141
Jenkins, Ambrose 62

Jenkins, Elizabeth (1886–1972), *mar. 1.* John H. Galer, *mar. 2.* John Barnett 62, 118
Johe, Carrie 108
Johnson, Alanson, *mar.* Sarah Alice Katherman 27, 32, 48
– Albert Williams, *mar. 1.* Dora Miller, *mar. 2.* Mary C. Steck 48
– Anna M., *mar.* S. C. Wilt 32
– Arminda (1849/50–1932), *mar. 1.* David Benny, *mar. 2.* Theodore Freed, *mar. 3.* J. M. Blankenship 32, 47, 53, 53, 65, 144
– Arthur F. 56
– Carrie 95
– Catherine Gertrude 32
– Charles 41
– Clayton 95
– David C. 32
– David Crawford, *mar. 1.* Hannah Mary Weikel, *mar. 2.* Mary Etta Ely 56, 64, 89, 96
– Eliza, *mar.* William Johnson 68
– Ella/Ellen, *mar.* William Johnson 66
– Elmer Elsworth 48
– Gainesville 41
– Grace M. (1888–1967) 56, 64
– Hannah, *mar.* William Johnson 95
– Harold B. 56
– Jennie 84
– Lewis M., *mar.* Isabelle Bertha Jolly 67, 73
– Lillian J. (1876–1944), *mar.* William Johnson 84
– Mary 32
– Maud (1882–1954) 56, 89
– Miles Warren 48
– Minnie Elizabeth 68
– Minnie Elizabeth May, *mar.* Boop 48
– Minnie Elva L. (1891/89–1961), *mar.* John Arthur Walls 60, 66-7
– Nellie Viola, *mar.* Bowersox 48
– Ray Lee 56
– Susie, *mar.* Showalter 48
– Walter C. 96
– William 32
– William 84

– William, *mar.* Hannah 95
– William, *mar.* Lillian J. 84
– William, *mar.* Catherine Switzer 32
– William, *mar.* Eliza 68
– William, *mar.* Ella/Ellen 66
– William F., *mar.* Anna Aumiller 40-1
Jolly, Allen Seymour, *mar.* Nancy Jane Zimmerman 14, 46, 49, 65, 66, 69
– Arthur 85
– Bertha Mae (1894–1981), *mar.* George Allen Landis 69, 85
– Charles Allen 85
– Clair F. 85
– Clarence Dale 86
– Edward. F. 47, 49
– Edward Thomas, *mar.* Mary Blanche Bracken 73, 81, 86, 89
– Florence 85
– Frank Seymour, *mar.* Eva Regina Hironimus 47, 50, 69
– Hattie Blanche (1879–1967), *mar. 1.* Thomas W. Sholter, *mar. 1.* Robert C. Tharp 47, 119
– Hilda May (1903–1981) 86, 89
– Isabelle Bertha (1899–1985), *mar. 1.* Jonas William Barnet, *mar. 2.* Preston B. Alexander, *mar. 3.* Lewis M. Johnson 73, 86
– Margaret N., *mar.* Weller? 47
– Martha L. 85
– Mary 49, 80
– Mary Adele 47, 103
– Melvin C. 47, 60
– Minerva May, *mar. 1.* William Henry Whatmore, *mar. 2.* William Kaler 47, 65
– Sarah Jane (1875–1967), *mar. 1.* John Stump, *mar. 2.* Ambrose Bettilyon, *mar. 3.* John Boop 47, 49
Jones, Amelia 83
– Mabel 83
Jordan, Diane, *mar.* Wagner 123
– Lily E. (1870–1923), *mar.* William F. Barnet 82
– Minerva (1865–1937), *mar.* Reed T. Pursley 59
– Richard 82

Index of Personal Names

Jordan, Sarah 82
– Scott R. 123
– Toni, *mar.* Dallas Klauger 123
– Tracy, *mar.* Buswell 123
Kahley, Carl E. 97
– Elmer Elsworth, *mar.* Mabel Irene Barnett 74, 96, 140
– Eugene F. 97
– John Jay 97
– Lois, *mar.* Sullenberger or Schellenberger 97
– Virginia J. (1919–1995), *mar. 1.* Owen W. Everett, *mar. 2.* Charles Dailey 97, 140
Kaler, also Galer
– Amelia Jane (1916–2004), *mar.* Robert Kermit Ely 114
– Elda M., *mar.* Marcinko 67
– Elizabeth, *mar.* Michael Kaler 38
– George 67
– Hannah 38
– John 67
– Mary 38
– Michael, *mar.* Elizabeth 38
– Milton E. 114
– Paul 67
– William, *mar. 1.* Minnie Elva Johnson, *mar. 2.* Minerva Mae Jolly 65, 67
Kanour, Eugene K. 130
– Nancy Ruth, *mar.* Spearing 130
– Paul Eugene, *mar.* Margaret Ruth Kurtz 130
Katherman, also Catherman
– see Aumiller, Ada E.
– John F. 48
– Sarah Alice (1855–1931), *mar.* Alanson Johnson 48
Keefer, Mabel 113
Keene, Elizabeth 54
– Herbert, *mar.* Carrie C. Sholter 54, 78
Keister, see Libby, Hattie
– see Libby, Marguerite
– see Styers, Phoebe
– David 80
– Earl 104
– Elmer J., *mar.* Ethel Border 104
– Florence, *mar.* Stamm 104
– George 9
– Harry Paul 104
– Helen, *mar.* Poeth 104
– Henry, *mar.* Catherine Shively 35
– Lydia 50
– Roland 80
– Samuel, *mar.* Catherine Shively 35
Kell, Betsy L. 92
Keller, Lottie 68
Kenee, Marlin 75
Kerstetter, Joyce 132
– Marlin 132
Kiehl, Margaretha 24
Kinney, see Pursley, Helen
Kirkhoff, Crystal Viola 138
Kissinger, Allen K. 113
– Elizabeth L. (1915–2003), *mar. 1.* Herman Reich, *mar. 2.* Harry Lee Snook 113
Klauger, Alma 136
– Charles W. 136
– Dallas 123
– Harold 91, 136
– Lewis W., *mar.* Catherine Delores Cooney 136
– Lewis W., Jr. 136
– Minerva Gertrude, *mar.* Clarence Frederick Umlauf 136
– William L. 136
Kleckner, Annie Minerva (1872–1918), *mar.* George Burns Hironimus 50, 82
– Lewis 82
– Richard 80
– S. 80
– Susan 80
Kline, see Sholter, Elvina
– Clara 71, 84
– Donald L., *mar.* Jane Elizabeth Beaver 122
– Donald S. 122
– Donna, *mar.* Jim Slaughter 122
– Harry 115
– Mary Lou (1925–2005), *mar.* Mrs. Jere L. Engle 115-16
– Patty, *mar.* Severn 122
– Robert Omer Curtis, *mar.* Rhoda Jeanette Hile 130

Kline, Ronald 130
– William F. 51
Klinger 71
Knauss, see Canouse
Knoble, N...., *mar.* George Oberle 99
Kobel, Ruth M., *mar.* Elery E. Newberry 132
Koonsman, Franklin C. 90
– Lottie Elizabeth, *mar.* Chester Rea Fox 90
– Ray Reynolds 90
– Reba C. (c. 1901/00–1945?), *mar.* Charles E. Wenrich 90, 109
– William W., *mar.* Cora C. Barker 90, 109
Korten, August, *mar.* Katarina Reich 104
Kreisher, Clarence Adam 52
– Cora May 52
– Eva Elletta 52
– George W., *mar.* Nancy A. 52
– Nancy A., *mar.* George W. Kreisher 52
– Regina Clare 52
Kreps, Arthur J., *mar.* Susan Alice Irwin 90, 91
Krick, Martha Jean (1916–2004), *mar.* Adam Martin Yocum 11, 121
– Maurice Hanson 121
Krumrine, John C., *mar.* Tome Elverta Hosterman 15, 48, 97, 106, 146
Kuhns, Hester 102
Kurtz, Margaret Ruth (1907–1997), *mar.* Paul Eugene Kanour 130
– Samuel Ira 130
Lahr, Cyrus H., *mar.* Bertha Ann Pursley 58
Lamey, Thelma (1920–1984), *mar.* L. Roy Himmelreich 125
Lamine, Grace V. 121
Landis, Clair 69
– George Allen, *mar.* Bertha Mae Jolly 69
– Kenneth Franklin 69
– Thelma 69
Latherow, see Schoening, Phyllis S.
Layton, Alfred Simon 115

– Velma Nadine (1910–1979), *mar.* Benjamin Thomas Goodlander 115
Leasure, James 75
Lepley, see Aumiller, Carrie Mabel
Levan, Jody P. 111
– William C. 111
– William E., Jr., *mar.* Pauline A. Crebs 111
Libby, Albert 36
– Asa 36
– Beatrice 112
– C. Clinton 112
– Charles 36
– Cora E. (1909–2003), *mar.* James Garrettson Price 61, 91
– Daniel Carey, *mar.* Ida Seymour Freed 36, 61 65, 88, 91
– Daniel C., Jr., *mar.* Sarah E. Hironimus 61, 105
– David, *mar.* Emma Jane McPherson 36
– David McKinly 64
– Dewey 61
– Donald Roger 105
– Ethel R., *mar.* Caldwell 105
– Francis C. 64
– George R., *mar.* Olive R. Miller 61, 112
– George R., Jr. 112
– Harold 105
– Harry Wade 112
– Harvey J. 64
– Hattie, *mar.* Keister 64
– Helen M. 112
– Ida 11
– Jack S. 105
– James L., *mar.* 1. Mary Lucinda Hironimus, *mar.* 2. Annie Elizabeth Hironimus, *mar.* 3. Ida Seymour Freed 44-5, 61, 64
– Jean L., *mar.* Boyer 105
– John 36
– John Russell, *mar.* Marian Rosella Canouse 64, 112
– Josephine E., *mar.* Mayes 105
– Katherine Virginia, *mar. 1.* Shaw, *mar. 2.* Martin 105

Index of Personal Names

Libby, Lyman 61
– Lyman 105
– Margaret or Marguerite, *mar.* Keister 61
– Marion S., *mar.* Prior/Priar 105
– Marjorie M., *mar.* Shively 105
– Mary E., *mar.* Swanger 64
– Mary Ellen 36
– Nancy, *mar.* Ney 105
– Paul William 105
– Phineas H. 64
– Ralph T. 105
– Roger 105
– Ruth L. 112
– Samuel 36
– Sarah, *mar. 1.* William Baylor, *mar. 2.* Lawrence Brouse 60, 64
– Theodore 61
– Thomas, *mar.* Ann Jane Pursley 36
– Thomas, Jr. 36
– Virginia Gertrude (1906–1989), *mar. 1.* Jonas W. Barnett, *mar. 2.* James Lester Bettilyon 61, 103
– W. Miller 112
– Wealthy, *mar.* Morrow 61
– William 36
– William Sherwood 11, 61
Lingle, Margaret 74
Leonger, Annie K. 57
Lomison, Kay 114
Long, Morris 51
Longer, Alvah W., *mar.* Mary M. Bettleyon 57, 94
– Amber M. 57
– Ambrose D. 57
– George E. 57
– James L. 57
– Lillie J. 57
– William A. 77
– William O. 57
Lundgren, see Goodlander, Bessie H.
Lynn, Henry 123
Lyons, LaRue Wallace 139
McCloskey, Mabel (c. 1886–1936), *mar.* Arthur C. Silvius 106
McColm, William, *mar.* Martha Harriet McPherson 39, 76, 81

McCurdy, Foster, *mar.* Elizabeth Schnure 35, 50
– Jennie 50
– Mary 35
– Samuel 35
– Susan, *mar.* Thomas McCurdy 35
– Thomas, *mar.* Susan 6, 33, 35
– Thomas 35
McMinn, Hazel G. 122
McPherson, Alda Lavina, *mar.* William Cromly 39
– Charles Milton 39
– Clarence Newton 39
– Cora Bella (1875–1954), *mar.* David P. Galer 39, 71
– Emma J. C. (1863–1950), *mar. 1.* William A. Pursley, *mar. 2.* David Libby 36, 39, 55, 58
– Isaac 39
– James Silverwood, *mar.* Sarah Catherine Sholter 39, 55, 71, 79
– Jane 81
– John Howard 39
– Maggie May 39
– Martha Harriet (1839–1914), *mar.* William McColm 39, 75, 81
– Mary Catherine (1861–1933), *mar.* David C. Galer 39, 78-9
– William, *mar.* Christiana Moore 76
– William 39
Magnuson, see Wintersteen, Sherry
Marcinko, see Kaler, Elda M.
Marston, Adda 38
– Alvah, Jr., *mar.* Elizabeth Galer 38, 57, 59
– Alvah, Sr., *mar.* Sara(h) Ann Pennington 38
– Charles 38, 57
– Eugene 59
– James 38
– Vesta 38
Martin, see Libby, Katherine Virginia
– Elizabeth Jane (1972–2006), *mar.* Kerry L. Wenrick 138
– John F. 138
– Sarah Ann 54, 60
Mayes, see Libby, Josephine E.

Middlesworth, Edna Mae 102
Miller, Andrew 34
– Dora 48
– Florence Alberta 127
– Hannah 34
– Hazel 127
– Jacob 34
– Leon Harrison, *mar.* Ida C. Hironimus 72, 83
– Mary (1786–1872), *mar.* Peter Miller 34
– Olive R. (1889–1983), *mar.* George R. Libby 112
– Peter, *mar.* Mary 34
– Rachal 34
– Rebecca 34
Mills, see Sholter, Sandra Lee
Milroy, Jean Dora (1928–2010), *mar.* John Herbert Aimetti 138-9
– Lyman Derr 138
Minium, Katie Leona (1938–2016), *mar.* Jimmy Robert Ely 111, 139
– Orval 139
Montague, Miriam A. (1905–1961?), *mar.* William Wilson 108
– William 108
Moore, Christiana 76
Morgan, see Yocum, Hilda Kay
– Mary A., *mar.* Robert S. Morgan 105-6
– Robert S., *mar.* Mary A. 105
Moyer, Daniel 25
– Ellen E. (1846–1918), *mar.* William Tate 76-7
– Margaret May (c. 1849–1916), *mar.* Lewis Shaffer 76, 99
– William 28
Munson, Hazel?, *mar.* Evald G. Edberg 106, 109-10
Nearhood, Catherine 96
Neidigh, see Pursley, Dorothy Mae
Neuhauser, George R., *mar.* Viola Regina Prosser 131, 137
– Helen (1908–1994), *mar.* William Earl Ammon 92, 98, 131
– Joseph 92, 98, 131
– Mary S. (1900–1975) 92, 98, 131

– Robert Leroy, *mar.* Armena Elizabeth Burkman 131
– Sadie C. (1897–1984) 92, 98
– Seth G. 137
– Victor, *mar.* Elizabeth M. Snyder Shaffer 98
Newberry, also Newbury
Newberry, Elery E., *mar.* Ruth M. Kobel 132
Ney, see Libby, Nancy
Oakes, see Spacht, Cora
Oberle, George, *mar.* N.... Knoble 99
– George 99
– Hilda 99
Oldt, David Michael 139
Osmond, Mary 42
Ott, Roy 91
Overt (Cavant), Ann 33, 37
Palensar, see Galer, Ethel
Pardoe, Jessie 87
Parsons, Jane (1817–1893), *mar.* David Galer 43, 59
Paskovich, Frank 133
Pavelic, Anna 126
– Barbara Louise (1918–2006), *mar. 1.* Michael S. Gaston, *mar. 2.* Edward T. Barnet 126-7
– John 126
Pearson, George 116
– Violet May (1919–2005), *mar.* James Glaus 116
– Zepha 116
Peck, Charles. *mar.* Mary 112
– Charles Jr. 112
– Edna 112
– Mary, *mar.* Charles Peck 112
– Samuel L. 112
– William O. 112
Pennington or Scribner, Sarah Ann (1814–1879), *mar.* Alvah Marston Sr. 38
Pick, Levi 128
– Nellie M., *mar.* Charles G. Rheppard 128
Plank, Adeline 131
Poeth, see Keister, Helen
Price, Carey G. 91

Index of Personal Names

Price, J. Travers 91
— James Garrettson, *mar.* Cora E. Libby 91
— Rosemary P. 91
— Thomas F. 91
— William L. 91
Prosser, Viola Regina (1916–2005), *mar.* George R. Neuhauser 137
— William Henry 137
Pursley, Aminda, *mar.* Glover 46
— Ann Jane (1848–1911), *mar.* Thomas Libby 31, 36
— Bertha Ann (1882–1956), *mar.* Cyrus H. Lahr 55, 58
— Blanche, *mar.* Jacob Charles Barnett 102
— Carrie 46
— Charles W. 59
— Clara A., *mar.* Boop 59
— David or Daniel 31
— David N. 72
— David R., *mar.* Clara E. Smith 46, 72
— Dorothy Mae, *mar.* Neidigh 75
— Eliza, *mar.* Helwig 46
— Elwood E. 75
— Harry R. 46
— Harry S. 75
— Helen 46
— Helen, *mar.* Kinney 75
— Helen E., *mar.* Harter 72
— James 3
— James C. 31, 39
— James Geddes 46
— James K., *mar.* Sarah Fietta Swank 46
— James L. 59
— James William 55
— John A. 59
— Joseph 31
— Marcus 31
— Mary C. (1850/42–*c.* 1868), *mar.* John Leroy C. Goodlander 31, 40
— Mary Ellen, *mar.* Crouse 46
— Mary L., *mar.* C. D. Cook 59
— Minnie Ellen, *mar.* Schreck 75
— Molly, *mar.* Haas 75
— Oscar A., *mar.* Carrie C. Sholter 54, 78
— Oscar C. 59
— Reed (Reid) T., *mar.* Minerva Jordan 31, 59
— Samuel A. 59
— Sarah 46
— Warren B. 59
— William 59
— William, *mar.* Carrie 46
— William, *mar.* Ruth May Hironimus 83
— William A., *mar.* Emma J. C. McPherson 55, 58
— William B. 31
— William P., *mar.* Eliza Switzer 31, 36, 39, 40
Quinlan, Jennie Virginia (1855–1934), *mar. 1.* John Leroy C. Goodlander, *mar. 2.* Thomas H. Eisenhuth 48, 68
Ranck, Lola Gwen 134
Reader, Alda May (1929–2001), *mar.* Ammon J. C. Shaffer 134
— Herbert Felker 134
Rearick, see Benney, MaryBelle
Reed, David, *mar.* Doris 132
— Doris, *mar.* David Reed 132
Reich, Herman, *mar.* Elizabeth L. Kissinger 104, 113
— Katarina (1872–1936), *mar. 1.* Reich, *mar. 2.* August Korten 104
— N.... 104
Reid, see Benney, Ida
Reinarin, Magdalena Maria 23
Reitz, Lillian 100
Renn, see Aumiller, Hattie Mabel
Reppert, Estella Elizabeth (1891–1974), *mar.* Elmer Reno Dauberman 45, 95
Repport, Alice 80
Rheppard, also Reppert
— Charles G., *mar.* Nellie M. Pick 45, 128
— John E., *mar.* Mary Aumiller Boop 45, 95
Rippel, Ethel (1905–1974), *mar.* Raymond B. Winter 121
— John E. 121
Riser, Dessie Jane (1908–1998), *mar.* Ray Kenneth Cronin 141

Riser, George F. 141
Rishel, E. Kauffman 101
Romich, John 32
Rote, Bertha 50
Rowe, Florence V. 111
Rowland, Priscilla 121
Ryan, Laura C. 141
Sampsell, Charles 59
– Susanna 93
Savage, Florence 83
Saxton, Mary Ann (1815–1885), *mar.* Abraham Freed 62
Schambach, see Spangler, Jill
Schneeberg, David 118
– Max, *mar.* Virginia Kathryn Ely 118
Schnure, Bruce 75
– Christian 50
– Elizabeth (c. 1841–1895), *mar.* Foster McCurdy 50
Schoening, Barbara L., *mar.* Frank Paskovich 133
– Clifford Clark, *mar.* Anne Wojeski 132-3
– Phyllis S., *mar.* Latherow 133
Schreck, see Pursley, Minnie Ellen
Schultz, Sarah E. 90
Schwenk, Bruce 129
– Carl N. 129
– David 129
– Shirley L., *mar.* Weand 129
– Wilmer Herbert, *mar.* Jennie Margaret Zimmerman 128
Scott, Aaron P. 133
– James, *mar.* Louise Goehring 133
– Mia L. 133
– Noah R. 133
Scribner, see Pennington
Severn, see Kline, Patty 122
Shade, Michael Thomas 139
Shaffer, Ammon J. C., *mar.* Alda May Reader 134
– Ammon John, *mar.* Bessie Margaret Hironimus 26, 66, 83, 98, 105
– Catherine 143
– Christian, *mar.* Margaretha Hironimus 24, 26
– Christian, Jr. 26

– Christine Beth, *mar.* Mann 134
– Donna Darlene 134
– Elizabeth M. Snyder (1912–1931), *mar.* Victor Neuhauser 98
– Jacob 26
– Janet Marie 134
– Lewis, *mar.* Margaret May Moyer 25, 26, 76, 99
– Mary 26
– Nancy 26
– Rachel Jane 99
– Sebastian 26
Shaw, see Libby, Katherine Virginia
– Laura C. 141
Shawda, Edward 70
Shearer, see Yocum, Nancy L.
Sheesley, Gary Lynn 139
Shields, Alice Catherine, *mar.* Charles W. Galer 31-2, 55
– Annie M., *mar.* Felix Shields 32, 54-5
– Felix, *mar.* Annie M. 32, 54
– John Elmer 55
– William Henry 55
Shirk, Abraham 29
– Angeline 29
– Catherine (1836–1896), *mar.* Jacob F. Barnet 29
– Elizabeth 29
– Jacob, *mar.* Eliza Goodlander 29
– Levina 29
– Susannah 29
– Samuel 29
Shively, see Libby, Marjorie M. 105
– Catherine (1803–1873), *mar. 1.* Henry Keister, *mar. 2.* Samuel Keister, *mar. 3.* William Bohnestiel 35
– Clark 47
– John 35
Sholter, Agnes Jane 51
– Alice 54
– Amanda 54
– Andrew 70
– Anthony James 77
– Asa Roland, *mar.* Verna Theora Erdley 78, 100, 107
– Benjamin F., *mar.* Agnes Jane Aikey 28, 51

Index of Personal Names

Sholter, Beverly 106, 110
– Carey Daniel 51
– Carrie C. (1877/79–1963), *mar. 1.* Herbert Keene, *mar. 2.* Oscar A. Pursley 54, 78
– Charles Dervin 77
– Chestia Alverta (1868–1943), *mar.* Harry A. Walls 60, 67, 145
– Cora Louise (1887–1970), *mar.* Simon Showalter Bingaman 63, 77, 117
– David Roland, *mar.* Heidelinde Havice 124
– Dorothy 100
– Edna M. 100
– Edward 77
– Edward L., *mar.* Clara E. Bartley 78, 99-100
– Ella V., *mar.* Morris Long 51
– Ellsworth 100
– Elvina, *mar.* Kline 51
– Fred 77
– Gail F., *mar.* Ulrich 119
– George J., Sr., *mar.* Janet Edberg 100, 103, 106, 110
– George J., Sr., *mar.* Sarah L. Galer 118
– George J., Jr. 119
– George Washington, *mar.* Elizabeth Minerva Buffington 29, 54, 78
– Grace, *mar.* Edward Shawda 70
– Guy 100
– Hannah M. (1844–1943), *mar.* Joseph L. Wallace 28
– Henry 28, 60
– Janet 100
– John Benjamin, *mar.* Kathryn Hironimus 70, 71
– John E., *mar.* Catherine Goodlander 7, 28, 39-40
– Jonas B. 77
– Joseph Lawrence 124
– Joseph Roland, *mar.* Jean Howell Adams 100
– Laurie Jean, *mar.* George Bloom 124
– Leona Lillian E. (1911–2013), *mar.* Benjamin H. Wirt 100, 107
– Margaret R. 28
– Martha Jane 28
– Mary Alice (1860–c. 1942), *mar.* William Stimeling
– Mary Elizabeth (1845–1902), *mar.* George O. Barnett 28
– Mary Elizabeth 77
– Mary E. (1881–1932), *mar.* John H. Barnett
– Mary Lou 103
– Patti Lee, *mar.* Melvin Drumheller 124
– Perry Clayton 54
– Ralph Clarence 51
– Rosella 100
– Ruth Viola (1897–1986?), *mar.* Kimber C. Farrow 70, 71
– Sadie, *mar.* Alfred File? 51
– Samuel 54
– Sandra Lee, *mar.* Mills 119
– Sarah Catherine (1833–1888), *mar.* James Silverwood McPherson 28
– Thomas W., *mar.* Hattie Blanche Jolly 54, 119-20
– William Charles, *mar.* (Margaret) Mary Salome Specht 28, 77
– William David 51
Shomo, Emma 62
Showalter, see Johnson, Susie
Showers, see Spangler, Lisa
– Betty, *mar.* Werren Wintersteen 121
Silvius, Arthur C., *mar.* Mabel McCloskey 106
– Miriam R., *mar.* Briggman 106
Sipe, see Aumiller, Sarah Mae
Skyler, Annie 106
Slagenwhite, Gertrude 108
Slaughter, Jim 122
Slotterback, Mollie C. 136
Smith, Abram 72
– Annie E. 67
– Clara E. (1874–1950), *mar.* David R. Pursley 72
– Edwin F. 67
– Irwin 80
– Sarah 56
Snook, Harry Lee, *mar.* Elizabeth L. Kissinger 113

Snook, Mathias 143
Snyder, see Goodlander, Harriet
– Alice Elizabeth
– Carrie M. (1876–1943), *mar.* William Reynolds Valentine 8, 106-7
– John Wesley 107
Solomon, Myrtle 125
Spacht, also Specht
– Anthony James 77
– Cora 74
– Jacob Franklin, *mar.* Amanda Christine Derr 60-1, 74
– (Margaret) Mary Salome (1857–1917), *mar.* William Charles Sholter 77
– Mary 74
Spangler, Jill, *mar.* Schambach 135
– Lisa, *mar.* Showers 135
– Orville L., *mar.* P. Joan Hanselman 134
– Steve Eaton 135
Spearing, see Kanour, Nancy Ruth
Speck, Catherine W. (1898–1963), *mar.* Frank E. Speck 129
– Frank E., *mar.* Catherine W. 129
Spinner, Susanna 24
Stamm, see Keister, Florence
Starr, Caroline 101
Staudinger, Irene Elizabeth (1908–1967), *mar.* Edward C. Galer 110
Steck, Mary C. 48
Steese, Franklin B., *mar.* Virginia Mae Engleman 125
Stevens, Elizabeth Emma 123
Stevenson, Margaret 67
Stimeling, Clemuel, *mar.* Agnes Jean Wallace 40, 58, 119, 127
– Florence Alberta 119
– Florence Bertha, *mar.* Charles Sampsell 59
– Lesta 119
– Wesley Reno 58
– William, *mar.* Mary Alice Sholter 58
Stoltzfus, Elizabeth 92, 98, 131
Stover, Henry Gast 109
Strauss, Mary Barbara 29
Strickler, see Barnett, L. Jane
Strunk, Rachel A. 79

Stump, John, *mar.* Sarah Jane Jolly 49
Styers, Mary 99
– Mary 80
– Phoebe, *mar.* 1. Keister, *mar.* 2. Zachary T. Galer? 11, 80
Sullenberger or Schellenberger, see Kahley, Lois
Swain, Richard 103
Swanger, see Libby, Mary E.
Swank, Sarah Fietta (1852–1933), *mar.* James K. Pursley 46
Switzer, Catherine (c. 1826–1883), *mar.* William Johnson 32, 53
– David 31, 52
– Eliza (1817–1896), *mar.* William P. Pursley 31, 36
– Elizabeth 31, 32
– Jane (1822–1886), *mar.* John Galer Jr. 31, 44
Tate, Annie M. 77
– James 77
– Margaret J. (1871/3–1915), *mar.* Ambrose D. Bettilyon 68-9, 87
– William, *mar.* Ellen E. Moyer? 76-7, 99
Teichman, Charles W., *mar.* Mildred F. Hironimus 75, 135
– Mary Elaine, *mar. 1.* Dohrmann, *mar. 2.* Genevish 135
– Seibert, *mar.* Connie Snook 135
Tharp, Robert, *mar.* Hattie Blanche Jolly 47, 119-20
Thompson, see Bilger, Pauline
– Katherine 68
Tyson, see Bilger, June
Ulrich, see Sholter, Gail F.
Umlauf, Clarence Frederick, *mar.* Minerva Gertrude Klauger 136
Valentine, William Reynolds, *mar.* Carrie M. Snyder 8, 106-7
Vandergrift, Victoria 138
Vonada, Rachel 97
Wagner, see Jordan, Diane
– Ralph 70
Wallace, Agnes Jean (1892/89–1959), *mar.* Clemuel Stimeling 40, 58, 119
– Amanda R., mar. William Young 40

Index of Personal Names 175

Wallace, Charles E. 40
– Job, *mar.* Nancy 57
– John Langton 40
– Joseph L., *mar.* Hannah M. Sholter 29, 39-40, 119
– Nancy, *mar.* Job Wallace 57
– Samuel 40
Walls, Dayton 67
– Harry A. *mar.* Chestia Alverta Sholter 60, 67
– John Arthur, *mar.* Minnie Elva L. Johnson 60
– Sarah Catherine 60
Watkins, Odessa 83
Weaser, Earl P., *mar.* Genevieve Friggle 120
Webster, Mary Ann 77
Weand, see Schwenk, Shirley L.
Weiand, Emmett 50
Weikel, Hannah Mary (1863–1895), *mar.* David Crawford Johnson 42, 56, 64, 89, 96
– Jamilla 28
– William 56
– William Eckley, *mar.* Jamilla Goodlander 42
Weiker, Adam 23
– Anna 24
– Catarina 24
– Catherina, *mar.* Jacob Barnet/Bernt 23
– Elizabeth 24
– George, Sr. 23
– George, Jr., *mar.* Maria (Mary) 23
– Hannah 24
– Jacob, *mar.* Mary Deal (Diehl) 24
– Jacob, Jr. 24
– Joseph 24
– Mahdelena 24
– Maria (Mary) (1770–1849/53), *mar.* George Weiker Jr. 23
– Peter 23
– Salome 24
– Samuel 23
– Susanna 24
Weinhoffer, Frank 129

– Kathryn Mary (1921–2001), *mar.* Michael Carl Zyry 129
Welch, see Wintersteen, Mary
Weller, see Jolly, Margaret N.
– Amelia 78
– Anna Minerva (1880–1963), *mar.* Harry Jefferson Greene 103-4
– Daniel O. 103
Wenrich, Charles E., *mar.* Reba C. Koonsman 90, 109
– Cora Lillian, *mar.* Henry Gast Stover 109
Wenrick, see Bilger, Caroline
– Derrick A. 138
– Kerry L., *mar.* Elizabeth Jane Martin 138
– Spencer A. 138
Wertz (Wuerz), Elizabeth, *mar.* Christian Goodlander 28
– Johann Dietrich 28
Wikel, see Benney, Laura
Whatmore, Anna Elizabeth 65
– Benjamin Allen 65
– Charles Sylvester 65
– Daisy Irene 65
– Estella Mae 65
– Franklin H. 65
– John Melvin 65
– Mary Helen 65
– Viola 65
– William Henry, *mar.* Minerva Mae Jolly 47, 65
Williams, Susan 48
– Ted 139
Wilson, Ruth Ann (1889–1940), *mar.* George William Bilger 13, 101
– William, *mar.* Miriam A. Montague 108
– William Benner 101
Wilt, Bessie Agnes 84
– Grace Dora 85
– Lee David 84
– Mary Ann 84
– Mildred 85
– S. C. 32
– Samuel 85

Wilt, Samuel Conrad, *mar.* Isabell Ann
    Aumiller 84, 93
– Walter Clarence 85
Wink, Lillie May 115
Winter, Raymond B., *mar.* Ethel Rippel
    121
Wintersteen, Alan 121
– David 121
– Gary 121
– Ginger, *mar.* Egnew 121
– Lee 121
– Linda, *mar.* Halley 121
– Mary, *mar.* Welch 121
– Robin 121
– Sherry, *mar.* Magnuson 121
– Timothy 121
– Werren, *mar.* Betty Showers 121
Wirt, Benjamin H., *mar.* Leona Lillian
    E. Sholter 87, 100, 107
– Connie, *mar.* Bastian 108
– Francis 108
Wojeski, Anne (1912–2009), *mar.*
    Clifford Clark Schoening 132-3
– Michael 132
Wuerz, see Wertz
Yocum, Adam Martin, *mar.* Martha Jean
    Krick 121

– Adam M. 122
– Carole J., *mar.* Bower 121
– Hilda Kay, *mar.* Morgan 121-2
– Nancy L., *mar.* Shearer 121
Yost, see Himmelreich, April
Young, William H. 40
Zechman, George Lincoln, *mar.*
    Charlotte Hironimus 91
Zeiter, Eva (c. 1778–1852), *mar.* Jacob
    Hironimus Sr. 24
– Johann Georg 24
Zettlemoyer, Blanche E. 125
Zimmerman, David 128
– Jennie Margaret (1910–2005), *mar.*
    Wilmer Herbert Schwenk 128
– Jesse 46
– Lizzie 45, 67
– Margaret 128
– Nancy Jane (1847–1931), *mar.* Allen
    Seymore Jolly 46-7, 49, 65, 69, 119
Zyry, Barbara Ann 130
– Michael Carl, *mar.* Kathryn Mary
    Weinhoffer 129
– Michael Roman 130
– Paul Raymond 130
– Robert Francis 130
– Ruby Louise 130

Emilie Freer Jansma has received honors as a local historian in both Union and Centre Counties. She was recognized for her work as the former Curator of the Koch Collection of historical pictures of Centre County and the Curator of the Doris and Jack Sapia historical negatives collection of the Centre Region. In Union County she received the Historical Society Award for Historical Preservation work.

www.ingramcontent.com/pod-product-compliance
Lightning Source LLC
Chambersburg PA
CBHW021842220426
43663CB00005B/373